CHILDHOOD
AT BRINDABELLA

CHILDHOOD AT BRINDABELLA

MILES FRANKLIN

My First Ten Years

Eden

EDEN PAPERBACKS
an imprint of Angus & Robertson Publishers

Unit 4, Eden Park, 31 Waterloo Road,
North Ryde, NSW, Australia 2113, and
16 Golden Square, London W1R 4BN,
United Kingdom

First published
by Angus & Robertson Publishers in 1963
Paperback editions 1974, 1979
Reprinted 1980, 1981
This Eden paperback edition 1987

Copyright Miles Franklin estate 1963

ISBN 0 207 15843 6

Printed in Australia by The Book Printer

Publisher's note

MILES FRANKLIN wrote this delightful autobiography in 1952-1953. She was unable to arrange for publication before her death in 1954, and the MS. came to Angus and Robertson Ltd from her executors, the Permanent Trustee Co. Ltd of New South Wales.

With the MS. she left two papers explaining how she came to write it. The first was a letter which apparently she intended to post with the MS. to Pixie O'Harris, but never got around to doing it; and the other, also explaining Pixie O'Harris's part in the affair, might have been intended as a draft for a foreword, but rather reads as if she jotted it down hastily just as a method of getting herself started on the book. It seems clear from these papers that she had intended to dedicate the autobiography to Pixie O'Harris, and this note should be taken as fulfilling her wishes in that respect.

The story told in the papers is simply that the well-known writer of Australian children's books, Pixie O'Harris (in private life Mrs Bruce Pratt), had urged Miles Franklin to write something of the same kind herself. Miles Franklin felt she couldn't do that; but she did feel she could describe her own childhood; and she wanted very much to do so, partly because, as she says in her first chapter, "No other spot has ever replaced the hold on my affections of my birthplace", partly because she had been reading some unhappy memoirs of childhood and wanted to show that those years could be, as hers were, supremely happy. In the "foreword", dated 14th August 1952, she wrote:

A moment ago Pixie called me to the telephone to exhort me to do a children's story. I rebelled: I loathe children's stories. My mother sedulously kept them from me because she herself as a child had suffered so from the sorrow and fates of the children in them: such horrors as Little Red Ridinghood being eaten by a wolf, and the two little ones that had to be covered by the birds when they died lost somewhere, and Jack and the Bean Stalk with the gruesome slitting of the Giants' stomachs! They were a fantasy of horrors with their starving match-girls and lost children. We had no starving match-girls, and a lost child called out the countryside for a hundred miles to the rescue.

"But," she added:

For a long time I have been intending to write down earliest memories to discover how many I retain clear-cut before my memory is too moth-eaten. I meant to do this as a diary for myself alone, as sailors in the doldrums erect full-rigged ships in bottles just because the mind is an instrument that sanity cannot leave idle. I must find some kind of exercise for a mind unused except on chores or with the triffle-traffle of housewives.

What a shy wild creature Miles Franklin was, for all her out-spokenness!—slight, breathless, her quick utterances flying away from her like birds, and her brown eyes, even while they sparkled with vivacity, glancing this way and that all the time like birds on the watch for a hawk. She suffered, so she says in this book, "agonies of stage-fright" in her public appearances. It is typical of the reticence which is said to have fallen upon her after the publication of her first novel, and its mixed reception from friends, relatives, critics and the public, that even in the present book, which is straightforward autobiography, she changed all the place-

names and named most of the people only by their initials—
"Aunt A." and "Mrs M'G.". Even her father, in one fantastic outburst of reticence (a phrase Miles Franklin might
have liked) is called, when a guest speaks to him at the
dinner table, not "Franklin"—and he could hardly have
been anybody else—but "F.".

Thereby Miles Franklin presented her publishers with a
problem. Would it be fair to her to try to identify the
places and people?

To a certain extent she herself answered the question.
She is always careful in the MS. to use the invented place-
name "Gool Gool" for the town where she sometimes
stayed with relatives (students of the "Brent of Bin Bin"
novels will notice the similarity with "Bool Bool" in that
sequence). But apparently she did not have a privately-
taken photograph of "Gool Gool" and in the illustrations
which she pasted into the MS. of the autobiography she
included a coloured postcard of the town, on which is
clearly printed the caption, "The Poplars, Tumut". So
"Gool Gool", on the author's own admission, is Tumut,
New South Wales.

This may have been a slip; and if so it is an amusing one.
But it is clear when she calls her father "F." (which in the
context must stand for Franklin, not Father) that she was
not seeking any deep concealment of the places and people
in this book; and on the whole, since she was certainly not
out to attack or injure anybody but to write about them all
with affection, it seemed fair to attempt an identification.
This was made possible by the help of Miss Ruby Franklin
Bridle of Sydney, a cousin of Miles Franklin, and a list of
places and people is accordingly printed as an appendix in
this book. A few stray remittance men and similar characters have been left, however, under the pseudonyms or in
the anonymity which Miles Franklin would have wished
for them. It is worth observing, since the place-names are

so confusing in all the Miles Franklin and "Brent of Bin Bin" novels, that "Ajinby", her grandmother's house in which Miles Franklin was born and in which she spent some of her happiest days, was really Talbingo station, at Talbingo, New South Wales; and "Bobilla", where Miles Franklin's parents lived during most of the period covered by this book, was an invented name for Brindabella station, at Brindabella, not far from the present city of Canberra. "Stillwater", correctly named in the book, the property to which her parents moved from Brindabella, was at Thornford, near Goulburn, New South Wales.

Miss Bridle was also able to elucidate one extremely confusing piece of geography in Chapter 13 where, talking about swimming, Miles Franklin says "Father had known the Murrumbidgee, the bigger river, from his boyhood. . . . On Sunday mornings when I was tiny he would take me for a walk on his shoulder by the river; and, unable to resist, would strip and plunge in." This makes it appear that the Murrumbidgee was somewhere near Brindabella, which it isn't; or else that Miles Franklin lived somewhere near the Murrumbidgee, which she didn't. The only river at Brindabella, apart from creeks, is the Goodradigbee. But what she means here is that her father, who was born near Yass, New South Wales, had known the Murrumbidgee *there*. The river in which he took the infant Miles Franklin swimming was the Goodradigbee. On the trapping of lyrebirds referred to in Chapter 19, Miss Bridle says that the hunters used to preserve the butts of the tails in alum. They blew the eggs and sent the shells to America with the tails.

Miles Franklin was too well known to need any introduction to Australian readers as a novelist; but perhaps it should be mentioned for readers overseas that she is best remembered for *My Brilliant Career* (published in Edinburgh in 1901) and *All That Swagger* (1936), both novels with a good deal of semi-autobiographical content, set in the countryside of the present autobiography; and that she acknowledged herself in a private conversation in 1954 to be the author of the "Brent of Bin Bin" novels—notably *Up the Country* and *Ten Creeks Run*—dealing with the same kind of country and country life. She left in her will a considerable sum of money to establish an annual literary prize which is known as the Miles Franklin Award and which is awarded to novels or plays "which must present Australian life in any of its phases".

Acknowledgment is made to *Southerly* and *Meanjin* in which extracts from *Childhood at Brindabella* have already appeared.

Contents

1

First recollection

NO other spot has ever replaced the hold on my affections or imagination of my birthplace, nor are any other incidents so clearly and tenderly etched in my memory as those connected with it. These jottings therefore concern life as I found it before my tenth year, near the completion of which my family moved to another part of the country.

Recollection began early and remains indelibly, partly no doubt because my mind and affections are tenacious, and also those early years were remote, isolated, a unit without disruptions or upheavals of any kind, a period before I had developed sufficiently for aspirations, fears, desires and rending discontents.

My earliest captured memory was at the age of ten months. It nagged me in a casual way, as flickering thoughts return at intervals over a lifetime until they can be used or else fade completely.

So one night I said to my parents, "I remember I had a red flannel nightdress the time I slept with Father in the end room at Bobilla."

Mother dismissed this as a notion. Father had no skill as a nursemaid. "You never slept with your father in your life."

"Yes, I did. I remember Father carrying me along the veranda. The wind blew the candle flame to one side, and it was cold, and I did not like it."

"A nice pair you and your father would be in the end room!"

The end room in those early bush homes was reached by traversing the veranda, and was firmly set apart as the guest chamber. The timber was all hand-cut, the houses designed to meet the requirements and resources of the moment and the skill of the builders. There was nothing Gothic or Tudor in their size or shaping. There would arise a row of rooms, three or four at most to begin. These would be dining-drawingroom combined, with the main or parents' bedroom opening out of it, and the extra room at the end. On each side of an entrance passage from the kitchen, we had a skillion, one room for the nursemaid and the other for the child above the nursling after he was weaned and thrust out by his successor.

But this is ahead of the design. The home where men first went to work up to their marriage would be a two-roomed hut comprising kitchen-livingroom and bedroom-storeroom. Callers camped in their own nap on the veranda in summer or beside the kitchen fire in winter. There was attached to this room another, a little smaller in depth and width, which was the fireplace. It would be constructed of stones and plaster, sometimes of bark or slabs with a lining of stones and mud. Beams across it carried the hams and sides of bacon or spiced beef and bullocks' tongues preserved by slow smoking, and protected from the weather by a hooped sheet of bark. Lower beams would support the kettles and camp ovens and three-legged pots for cooking. The roof would be of stringybark on ridge poles with

2

a good steep pitch and held on by riders, snug and weather-proof if the trees from which the bark was stripped were carefully selected. The sheets of bark were often much larger than those of galvanized iron which succeeded them. Under this was a loft for flour, rice, sugar and other com-modities brought by bullock team once or twice a year.

In the tall-timbered country these homes were of slabs split and adzed from the imperial mountain-ash or stringy-bark trees and set in wall- and ground-plates that would remain sound for generations. Such homesteads increased like bulbs, in clusters. Often the bride would come to live in the hut to await a grander house, or would never expect any other.

In more pretentious cases the man would not bring his bride till the new house was up. This was the case with my father. The first erection had earthen floors, and its general room remained as a kitchen with the room off it turned into a storeroom-pantry, and others in the original row becoming the storeroom-greater where lurked the beef cask, bags of salt, the "washing-machine", the side-saddle and other odds and ends. This, as well as the room on its end, contained a bunk with blue blankets for working men and their callers. The kitchen was always set at a distance from the main house in case of fire. The house proper would grow in the same way, and when the end room fell to the bigger girls, another was added for the boys, and yet another for visitors. The veranda would stretch in accord-ance to be blocked at the ends by tiny rooms. Later these would serve as the station post office or office.

The main homestead at Bobilla was so elongated that a visiting uncle exclaimed, "Gosh! it will soon reach the river." The river was several hundred yards distant.

Other homesteads would consist of huts that sprang up all over the place—commodious places with wide hearths for grand fires in winter. Magnificent hardwoods stood all

3

about, and the energy of young men who desired a room to themselves was boundless. There were no radios to sap time. They enjoyed their own company where they could tell smokingroom tales without risk of waking the babies or shocking the ladies—who, by the way, could not be shocked, and knew all the stories, which seeped out through husbands.

On her marriage my mother came to a new house roofed with shingles of mountain-ash—as durable as English oak —capably split and sawn in uniform length, left to weather and put on with such craftsmanship that a leak was unknown. Its end room of my earliest memory was on our small unexpanded house. It was dedicated to guests, and knew mostly old gentlemen with grey beards in tweed suits, who cleared their throats with a note of authority; but occasionally there were beautiful young women in tight riding-habits, sometimes bowler hats, sometimes billycocks, with white or black veils to protect fair skins from sun or flies. It was the extraordinariness of a night in this special room and the unpleasant reason for such procedure that stuck in my memory.

The red nightgown and the candle flame in the wind plus something disagreeable in the experience clung, for usually an excursion with my father was the joy of my life.

"Father did take me to the end room. I can see the red nightgown. I didn't want to go with him. I cried, but Mother wouldn't come."

"I know!" said my father. "She's right! I took her there when she was weaned."

My father's memory was capacious and irrefutable till he took it with him to the grave in his eighty-fourth year.

"Nonsense!" repeated Mother. "She was weaned at ten months. She couldn't possibly remember it."

"Why not? I'm sure I can remember from my first year. There have been instances, why shouldn't this be another?"

4

"She has heard us talking about it and thinks she remembers."

Father became the persistent one. "She would hardly have heard us talking about her red nightgown and the candle flame. I don't remember ever mentioning her weaning to anyone since it happened."

Father tested my assertion. I remembered little more, but to this day usually retain a clearcut sense of place and direction. Forty or fifty years later I have astonished old hands by indicating "as good as a surveyor" where there had been trees, gates, tracks or other objects long ago. In one case I stated that, when in my third year, I had crossed a river at a certain spot after a night at W.'s and had turned to the left to continue on our homeward way. My surviving elders said the crossing had always been in another place. A man with a memory equalling my father's came: he thought a while and said, "By Jove! she's right. I recall it clearly now."

The end rooms were usually furnished with a double bed and a single to meet varying requirements; and I recalled, "We were in the big bed with the head of it to the wall beside the door."

"The double bed was along the far wall opposite the door," said Mother.

"But don't you remember the day we had to change their positions because you said you could get to the window easier past the single bed?"

That memory would seem to be a fact. Others of the time are not so precisely placed by such an incisive experience as weaning.

2

Being naughty

THE first memory of an uninhibited ego must have been little after the weaning for I cannot recall talking, and I talked and walked at twelve or thirteen months.

We were at Sunday mid-day dinner, with Father carving copiously from a big meat dish. Mother sat around the corner serving the vegetables. I was tied in my high chair near the corner between them. I could never be banished from adult company. The table was full, as usual at week-ends. There was an old remittance gentleman; and, prominent in my recollection, my grown-up cousin Joe, son of Father's eldest sister. He lived in loneliness many miles away in the scrub where he was clearing land secured under the Free Selection Act, which compelled residence.

I must have been below the age when Mother allowed her offspring to eat meat. An egg was my meal. I remember the egg and the spoon. Egg-spoons had rather long handles and were the shape of mustard-spoons. I must have clamoured for beef. Mother admonished, Father proffered bribes, but I disrupted the occasion. I would not eat that egg upon either persuasion or order. No egg, then no pudding, which was a treat. Finally Mother said if I did not eat the egg I should not be allowed to play with Joe after dinner, a real deprivation. Mother called on Joe to back her in this. The gentle Joe, shy to self-obliteration, thus cornered said, "Eat the egg, like a good girl, then we will go to see the chickens as soon as dinner is over."

My undeveloped subconsciousness must have resented the pusillanimity of Joe, thus to forsake me in public when in private he was an unresisting slave. I up with the laden spoon and flung it at him across the spotless Sunday napery —the only time I have ever been capable of so rousing a prima donna demonstration. Mother was aroused to extreme measures.

"Hoity-toity! She must be whipped—yes, *whipped*!"

Father's placations, Joe's supplications were swept aside.

"She must be taught self-control!" I never knew my mother to lose hers. "She must be corrected for her own good and the safety of society."

Mother had me on her hands. Father had Mother and me. He was driven to act, for there was never any divided authority between them.

"She must be switched."

This was mother's version of the honoured "correction by birching". She believed in a sharp switch stripped of leaves and applied round the calves of the legs where it could sting without risk of injury. Boxing of ears or any hitting about the body of a child was not to be thought of, nor vulgar threats such as some parents hurl at their young.

The switch, in this instance a twig from the table decorations, was laid across the back of my hand and wrist. It was a first experience in an outrage on my person which no monarch could have more furiously resented. I have no recollection of pain from the switch, but have a clear picture of its marks pink across my wrist and fist, and

7

noted for the first time the crease as if a string were tied in dough that separated the fat infant hand from the arm. The sight so affected me that I "reared up and broke the bridle" in the idiom of the time and place. I stiffened my spine, yelled and thrust myself into space regardless of consequences, the normal act of spirited infants. The chair was grabbed, its cargo unpinned.

Mother must have been embarrassed and helpless before company. The distressed and forgiving Joe's arms must have been ready, for I remember, "Take her away, Joe! Give her to the men. We don't want her here."

I remember being with Joe in one of the bunks at the end of the hayshed which were kept for working men or other callers who might be crowded out of the household rooms. I remember Joe cutting my fingernails to hold my attention . . . as the early navigator Flinders on one historic occasion lathered and shaved the Aborigines to divert them till his gunpowder dried.

I fell asleep and later was restored to society without any disturbing recollections, any realization of ignominy wiped away by the unselfish Joe. And that was the only corporal punishment I underwent from that day to this. I loathe all beatings, canings, beltings, blows and such violence, not so much for the pain that may be inflicted on the culprit as for the degradation of thus violating the separate private person of a fellow being, which involves the one who lays on the birch or cat in an experience as coarsening of his fibre as it is brutalizing to the receiver.

3

Late hours and baldness

I WOULD never close an eye before midnight. The nurse-maids available were little more than children, healthy creatures used to going to bed at dark, and could not be kept awake to "mind" me. The burden was little short of a scourge to people who bedded early after ceaseless and often violent physical activity, to whom ten o'clock was a late hour except when there was special company. I was a problem; but no problem except old age ever vanquished my mother.

Among first impressions are winter evenings with the room, as it appeared to me, brilliantly lighted by the grand log fire in the snowy hearth, the kerosene lamp on the round table in the corner with an unfurled peacock tail behind it like a wall panel of fabulous brocade, and my mother at the piano with two sperm candles in their wrought brass holders. These as I grew older seemed to me of pure gold such as the angels would have in their harps. I too sat at the piano. No lap, no pair of arms could lure from that position, when my mother began to play the instrument. This also must have been early, as I could not talk then—and I could say nearly any word in the dictionary at two. Also by eighteen months I would have been amenable to discipline and forbidden such rakish hours. Mother was firm in plan, particular in habits. Times of bedding and rising, meals, week-end routine were adhered to with precision. Mother was too well-regulated and capable for unpunctuality.

I was in my long robes—whether the infant robes, from which we were "short-coated" at three months, were resuscitated as evening wear, there is no one left to ask; but I would be correctly and daintily dressed. My mother enforced and ingrained a fastidiousness in me, so that later the frowsy habits of others caused me acute discomfort.

Mother was not musical, but she had been stiffly governessed, and played the piano correctly and was a prodigy in her situation. As part of her wedding paraphernalia she brought to the wild gullies the novelty of a sewing-machine and the social glory of a piano. The (pre-fire) Broadwood in a beautiful rosewood case had to come in by bullock dray, in some places down wriggling creek beds instead of tracks. Its survival with no scratch on it in such a passage was due to the resourcefulness, tough muscles, experienced bush-craft and tireless enthusiasm of young men serving a divinity.

My mother was the wonder of her region. She was beautiful and accomplished, clever as a hostess and in all departments of home-making. My father's pride in her was as a poem and a triumph combined, and sustained him to the end of his days. There was open expression of surprise as to how he could have carried off such a prize, but he too must have been irresistible with his slim straight height, his equestrian fame, his blue eyes, dark hair and sharp classical profile, his exuberant and witty though unbarbed humour, his boundless generosity. He was prized by all his contemporaries as "white throughout".

Young women were worshipped on the remote stations when men were many and women a rarity. Any normal woman with health and youth, whether in kitchen or drawingroom, was a magnet.

In the drawingroom on Saturday nights Mother would go through her "pieces" culminating in "The Maiden's Prayer", which was the gem of any genteel finishing school's repertory. Half-a-dozen men, and frequently more, formed an appreciative audience. Old songs would be sung, while in kitchen or hut men without women and without accompaniment would sing songs from song books interspersed by solos on concertina, jews' harp or mouth organ. Among the guests sometimes would be a player, and that would be a treat indeed.

A guest I remember from later, after a mine broke out a few miles away, was a once-distinguished musician by the name of Hopkins, whose uncle appeared in the book of *Hymns Ancient and Modern* as a composer. The poor little nephew, a victim of drink, had thought to repair his fortunes by picking up gold in Australia. Mother used to grieve for his fingers, swollen and cracked in the harsh frosts of our highlands, and bind them with ointment made by her grandmother. Father invited him to spend his leisure with us. It was a miracle, with his hands in such a state, that he could still bring music from the piano, which delighted him by its violin tone. Delirious with alcoholic poisoning, or what passed as alcohol where he was the prey of a shanty grog-concoctor, he would get astray trying to find our home in the dark and howl like a dingo till Father rescued him with coo-ees and a lantern. Once in delirium tremens he rushed in and hid under Mother's bed to be safe from the demons of his imagination that were chasing him. Mother met the situation with dignity and kindness till the men came home in the evening. But indeed he grew normal as soon as Mother sat him to the piano.

Other similar incidents were always met with sympathy and sanity, so that by force of early example I still feel obliged to do something for any drunk I find helpless in the streets.

Men would make to mother if sick or injured. Her presence seemed to comfort them, and she was as competent as a trained midwife or nurse. She could set clean breaks in bones with deftness and surety so that the doctor would find nothing to do but congratulate her. On one occasion she successfully sewed on a toe that a boy had severed from his brother with a tomahawk.

My grandmother tried to break me of the abnormality of late hours but must have failed, for tales remain of me on her silken lap playing with her watch chain and sticking my word in, often disconcertingly, at hours out of bounds for infants. When I was full grown, one of my mother's cousins journeyed to see me—out of curiosity, he said, to find out how an infant had developed who had sat complacently on his Aunt Sarah's lap when he would rather sneak by and camp under a bridge than meet her questionings as to what kind of a lad he was becoming.

Coupled with my inability to sleep before midnight was a compensating habit of sleeping till noon next day. I could not be awakened at normal hours, so the cot would be wheeled out of the room while cleaning went on with no concessions to keeping me quiet. In my early years I was so impervious to noises of any kind that there were fears that I was deaf. Hullabaloos were raised, loud bellowings by strange voices, bullock bells rung at my ear without winning any attention from me. At length my father let a heavy stone fall on the hardwood boards which wrung a start from me.

Oh, that such blessed indifference to noise had continued! No degree of fatigue will induce sleep in me if there is the smallest intrusive noise. Though I have been healthy beyond most in other departments of physical being, living has been embittered and reduced to frailty, and efficiency ruined, by an unconquerable sleeplessness.

A second abnormality must have been an embarrassment to my unfortunate parents. I was born as bald as an ostrich egg. Not a hair. My scalp was exceptionally healthy, no cradle cap, no flaw of any sort, and it has remained healthy through many years of hard and careless usage. The face and features given to the full moon were mine exactly. Months passed without sign of a hair. My head was scanned minutely and caressed with a brush as soft as silk, without response. My parents discussed the necessity for a wig when I should be older.

"Such a misfortune for a child, especially a girl!"

Happily Mr Shelley arrived. Little more remains of him than the Person from Porlock. The depth of my mother's anxiety and the hope he brought were embalmed in constant repetition of the story. Mr Shelley dismissed the probability of continuing baldness.

"The child has a perfect scalp and such an unusually beautiful skin that a complexion of unmatched perfection is promised. My sister was bald like that as a baby. She stayed bald till she was twelve months old. Then there was some soft down. Hair soon followed to such an extent that when she was seventeen my sister could sit on a chair and cover herself to the floor in her tresses."

Blessed Mr Shelley of treasured memory, who had a hairy sister!

At the end of the first year I followed Miss Shelley's lead. Seventeen was the goal. I never attained to quite Miss Shelley's length, but at seventeen I triumphantly sat on a footstool covered to the floor with womanly glory. It was never more than forty-three inches in length, but was extraordinary in other ways. It was among the finest I have known, a detraction which has made me envy women with coarser hair. At the beginning mine would curl softly at the ends but the weight soon held it straight. There were clouds of it. Washed in a strong hot solution of washing soda—the only shampoo ever used on it—to take out some of the natural oil, and plaited to put a wave in it, it made a mat that was spectacular and unmanageable. It was a marvel that it all could be rooted on one head, and it kept a clean line, never encroaching on the forehead or straying down the neck. It shone as if dressed with brilliantine, light brown which darkened to coppery tints after twenty. It could be controlled only be severe plaiting and its resilience made it as difficult to keep a ribbon on the end as it is to hold a silken shoe-lace from slipping. It was a nuisance and a physical handicap. Strange as it may seem today, when hair is closely cut, not alone for comfort but for beautification, long hair was considered a glory. No matter if it had to be piled in ungainly stacks, it attracted like a banner. Other girls could be glaringly handsome but Godiva Locks could cause an eclipse like a peacock unfurling his tail.

To say the best of it, it was not so abnormally produced as duck bills, or elongated necks or the steatopygia cultivated in Hottentot beauties, nor the distorted feet and hirpling gait induced by the smart shoes in our own shops.

4

Breathing

BREATHING was an epic discovery.

I was sitting before a glowing fire early one morning putting on my stockings. Mother was busy elsewhere. A slight chill would account for my being allowed the slackness of dressing at that late hour beside the fire. There were no muggy appearances in dressing-gowns in my mother's day and family. One bathed, dressed and combed completely before inflicting one's presence on one's fellows.

My nasal tubes were stopped and caused the phenomenon of snuffling. My nose wouldn't work! We were carefully overlooked so that we did not breathe through our mouths, nor wear those cavities open during sleep or at other times when they should be closed—firmly closed too. Looseness in living was not then generally esteemed and a slack mouth was discouraged as an inauspicious augury.

Mother did not quite understand the core of my distress. "Blow your nose! Like this!"

This brought no relief. An obstruction remained. I was overtaken by a devastating fear. Was I going to die like

15

the cats and dogs that were shot or poisoned? The thought of death remains dismaying to this day. The cackles of the nursemaid and my mother's exhortations failed to comfort because they were not explanatory.

Fortunately Uncle Hil arrived. He had lately married my father's sister Aunt Ignez. He was of English parentage with the endearing manner of those who long ago were *non Angli sed angeli*. Though not lacking intelligence and exuding common sense, he was a man of simple thoughts who retained a beautiful wonder about Nature in the form of all her living creatures. He loved flowers and was at one with animals. The working bullocks followed his instructions contentedly. He was the dear delight of all small children and had a repertory of tricks, such as seizing our noses and making them reappear in the form of his thumb between his own fingers till we'd shriek in thrilled delight and apprehensively feel our faces. He would play hide-and-seek and other games with us while others yarned about station affairs or argued politics by the fire or on the veranda. Blue-eyed and deliberate of movement, he was at peace with all men, even Aunt Ignez, who was a worrier and sometimes cantankerous. He contemplated the mysteries of life rather than grizzling to reform living or rebelling against it.

When he arrived on this day he put aside his business to unravel the cause of my discomfort and alarm. I must have been in my third year because of my size in relation to the little block I sat on, a present from Uncle Hil. He took up the case seriously, on my level, physically and mentally. He sank to his hunkers beside me, a bushman's habit he retained on the most unexpected occasions.

I snorted and puffed to show the cause of my worry. I was distressed by a noise like a toy bellows. Uncle Hil demonstrated so that I could hear him inhale and expire. From this I early became conscious that men breathe more audibly than women. Sit in a room in silence with men and women, and you can always hear the men breathing. I could detect the presence of a man in a room in darkness by this proclivity, and once was contemptuously amused by a burglar breathing like a chaff-cutter while bending over me to detect if I was sleeping, though otherwise he moved softly. I nearly pulled his moustache in ridicule, but that is a more grown-up recollection.

Uncle Hil's diagnosis gave complete satisfaction. I recall only the effect of his words. He too breathed, just as I did; everybody did.

"Everybody! Even Grandpa?"

"Yes—even Grandpa." Uncle Hil confirmed this in his deep rumbling bass voice with a merry laugh.

"Even the baby?"

"Yes, the baby too."

"Everything?"

"Yes, even the cattle, and the horses, and the sheep, and the cats and old Billy the goat and the dogs."

He soundly implanted in my avid empty noddle that we lived by this process, we would die only when it ceased. Such an avalanche of basic knowledge engrossed me. I took up consciously the act of breathing and have clung alertly and tenaciously to it ever since. Uncle Hil's handling of my problem long ago put him ahead of some of the patter-by-rote standardized psychiatrists of today.

5

Perambulator a sinecure

THE rhythm of horses came to me earlier than walking. In those moments—rare with me—when the sense of actuality has been slightly loosened by over-fatigue or a high temperature, there recurs for ever like the movement of a stream or the pattern of leaves flickering in a zephyr, the sensation of a well-bred horse being released, or about to be released, into action. Unforgettable are the pleasant odour of the warm satiny skin and the noble animal's every sensitive gesture as he waited a-tingle. He might rub his head on his fore-leg or stamp against a fly, test or mouth the bit, his alertness firmly reined to endure the finishing touches of departure. Then off, the instant the weight was on him, settling to the required gait as he cleared his breathing with a ruffle of good-will and good-going in his skilled responsibilities.

Deeply etched are the proportions of a tall easy horse controlled by a slim tall man with a natural beard and a very small child bundled on a pillow in front of him. The man was my father, one of my maternal uncles or one of Mother's cousins. The pillow, made by Mother, was stuffed

18

with feathers in an outer case of purple sateen of the kind used for dress-linings.

Except on the rarest occasions we went about on horses —horses that *were* horses, with a dash of blood—the walers so much sought for the Indian Army. My father and his brothers bred horses of full stature. The eldest brother had scorn for what he dismissed as "dunkies". A pony was a rarity among us. We liked to be up out of the water or bogs of the spring-heads and streams of our domain. The men rode far and fast: the children could not have kept with them on mere ponies.

My confidence and pleasure in horses was inborn. Mother rode seventy miles or more two months before I was born, from Bobilla to Ajinby the long way round. She went by impossible tracks negotiable only by a mountain-bred horse, at such angles that those unaccustomed could not retain a seat. For miles the horse plunged to the girths in snow. She rode her own blood horse, Lord Byron, who had borne her to her new home as a bride. His shoes had not been removed and snow collected in hard balls in the arches of his hoofs. Mother never forgot that punishing journey. There would have been fewer jolts had Lord Byron shed all his stilts at once, but he went off one at a time, and no surety from which point the next jerk would come, which increased the strain. She rode too on a hard new side-saddle in an elegant habit, tight-fitting and boned.

She was so exhausted at the end of the first gruelling day of over thirty miles that she had to rest for three days at the home of a selector. The motherly wife won Mother's unfading love, though I do not know that they ever met again. Mrs H. had the usual pioneer brood herself. She put Mother in her own bed as the warmest place for her bruised body, and placed her youngest, a child in arms, at Mother's feet to keep them warm.

When I was three months old Mother rode home by a

different route over the daisied plains by the sparkling rivulets where some of our longest creek-rivers began. My second uncle, a capable and humorous young man, carried me before him on the purple pillow. He says that I yowled when I grew hungry and the dairy, as he expressed it, had ridden too far ahead. Thus—straight from the bed in which I was born to the back of a horse with no perambulator intervening.

There was no gangway for prams in our bailiwick. My parents' home was a mile or more from the main homestead of my father's second brother, and his more advanced family. Between was little level track that took no heed of a creek or a fence or a swamp where the wild ducks used to "sing their long-drawn note of revelry rejoicing at the spring." And why would people of any age be pottering along on foot when there were horses of varied accomplishments for all?

But sometimes on Sunday afternoons the two families met half way on foot as a little company for the two young mothers and a change for the men from constantly catching and saddling horses. On such occasions I rode on my father's shoulder. No head so much as poked out of doors unhatted. Sunstroke was considered more likely than snakebite and when my father took off his hat to get it out of my way I desperately spread my fat paws on his crown to save him from death.

Nevertheless I had a perambulator, a beauty, fit associate for the sewing-machine and the piano. A young lady of my mother's standing was not loosed into marriage without all bridal equipment, though of course the pram came after, a gift from my famous little maternal great-grandmother.

The perfection of the vehicle was recalled to my mind recently by a picture in a London paper of the perambulator used by Queen Victoria, the pattern of which must have persisted in far-flung colonies into the eighties. The

Queen's was for two children and had a fringe on the canopy but in the picture was otherwise similar. No doubt it was grander, but mine was excellent. It had a hood of umbrella-like spokes that could be up, down or half-mast like the hood of a single-seated buggy. It was upholstered in red leather with a seat and foot-place swung low for a tot to step into it. The occupant sat in it as in a landau: it was useless to an infant who had not mastered her backbone. I do not remember having sat in it. Like other possessions of Mother's it was preserved in mint order during the nine years of my acquaintance, when my mother gave it away, and no doubt it sank in the world like a private carriage reduced to a "growler" for hire.

6

Choice of residence

AT the age of two I determined to live in the old home where I had been born. I much preferred life with my grandmother to that at Bobilla. I loved my grandmother's home above my own out of all proportion. I was passionately and unweanably attached to Ajinby. It was a family head station, a place of maturity and amenities. Bobilla was in the making, and my mother must have passed on to me her own dismay.

At the age of fifteen a reversal in fortune had taken her from the school-room and the home she loved, as I loved Ajinby. Her heart turned longingly towards it to the end of her days. Thereafter she had had to take the leading share in nursing her father, a man over six feet tall, paralysed and blind, a task beyond her strength. In addition she had had to labour as hard as a gardener, a farm hand, laundress, charwoman and general servant combined to retrieve the homestead at Ajinby from a pigwallow. It had been erected as a wayside inn in digging days and when my grandma and family had moved in, one of the doors was hanging on the hinges and pigs were comfortable in the earth of the unboarded floors. The roof had been leaky, bedbugs rioted throughout. Grandma and her children, some of them still infants, had converted it into the home I adored, long so famous for its hospitality, comfort, refinement and joyous associations that up and down the land its name has been perpetuated on numerous cottages by those who at some time had known its charms. My eldest uncle aged nine, under Grandma, had had to be working manager, bullock driver, cattle man, etc. The second uncle, aged six, had somewhat lighter work. As he remarks today, "A child was quite a fellow at six, and by nine he was an old man."

He was given the lighter task of going to town twenty-four miles distant with a pack-horse on errands and to supplement supplies in the winter when the unmade tracks were impassable for drays or carts. The horse he rode would also be loaded. My great-aunts have told me that his head could just be seen above the rolls on the pommel. It was difficult to mount among such impedimenta. In Uncle's words,

"I had to get the old nag beside a fence and first climb it and then clamber on from there."

Tales remain of his heroism in days of storm and boggy roads when the packs would slip and he had to walk in tall thick bush to some distant settler to have them replaced.

"I never forget that confounded old pack-saddle. It wasn't properly balanced and would always roll. Mother got it cheap because we had no money and she would never go in debt."

At home there would be anxiety and running far down the road at all hours, wondering and fearing what might have befallen the child that he was late in returning through swollen streams, one of them a swift river to be crossed by punt. In addition to the gruelling labour, my grandmother maintained the standing of the English better classes

23

and insisted upon her daughters observing the conventions and niceties of well-brought-up young ladies. In the taming of the Australian bush the pattern was the English squire. My mother's technique remained unflawed through all the grinding and tragic vicissitudes of a long, impecunious, unrewarded existence. She loathed the early hardships, restrictions and often complete isolation of Ajinby: to be removed to Bobilla, even more secluded, and wilder, with all its amenities to be introduced and maintained by herself, with the cruel burden of unrestricted child-bearing added, was too much.

At Bobilla I had competition with my own sisters and brothers, and my cousins, who were older and of greater physical hardiness and daring. At Ajinby I reigned alone among six young uncles and aunts, with my grandmother at their head. I grew up with pride in and unwavering affection for my grandmother, aunts and uncles. My satisfaction in them assumed a different character with maturity but it never waned, never was wounded. In my estimation my grandmother equalled God, with benificent resources and powers, and my aunts and uncles ranked as seraphim and cherubim. She had authority and self-reliance gained in running the whole station from the time the eldest of her children had been fifteen years old and she in a more hampered position than a widow's with her husband blind and helpless from an injured spine.

She was not quite five feet tall and composed of energy, determination, generosity, common sense, honesty and courage. She believed God to be a fixed identity as delineated by the Church from the Bible. She never owed a penny or turned a tramp from her door without replenishing his tucker-bags or giving him care if he were ill. She mothered the "godwits" by patching their clothes, giving them boots and admonishment. She was ceaselessly industrious, had a head for business and was known as a "good manager". Her haysheds and other storehouses were always well-stocked for winter with the yield from her orchards, potato and pumpkin paddocks, her fowlhouses, her dairy and vegetable garden. She grew and cured her own bacon as well as her own beef. Her streams were full of native trout and Murray cod. Order, plenty, decency, industry and hospitality were in the home I so loved.

My aunts and uncles have told me that I was a little tin god among them. To be the petted toy in such circumstances was paradise to the infant ego, and no doubt accelerated precocity.

My youngest uncle rode me on his shoulder, when he must have still been in his teens, where I would cling to his fair curls and shriek with apprehension when he rubbed a stubbly chin on mine and asserted that I would have a beard. I used to feel my face gingerly for signs and refer to Grandma. "Such nonsense! Teaching the child to tell lies," she would exclaim.

She reared her family in unbroachable rectitude with no concessions to weaknesses of the flesh. They were more than ordinarily intelligent and capable, yet free from either self-indulgence or wishy-washiness. In that home there was no bawdiness concerning physical functions. Disorder, profanity, drunkenness, gluttony, vulgarity and cruelty were undreamt by me there.

Grandma "fell into flesh" in her fifties and was advised by the doctor to take more exercise in the open air. Walking for walking's sake would have bordered on the sin of idleness, so she extended her gardening activities with my undetachable aid. I must have been very young to be so silly as to follow her and pick the seedlings out like a magpie as she set them. She threatened me with her hoe and I retreated wagging my head to remark sombrely, "I believe you really will kill me some day, Grannie, if you are not careful."

Grandma sped inside to tell my aunts. She rarely did anything except with the churning energy of a dynamo. She got as much of the prescribed exercise in this way as with the hoe, for she found my absurdities amusing and could not wait till later to retail them. A delectable situation for a lively child. I have no memory of ever having been left alone, or frightened, or being cold or unhappy. As nurses, tutors, playmates, friends, I had a vital group of near relatives who attended me for pleasure and affection, not for pecuniary reward. The attitude towards my fellows thus developed in me has never been fully overlaid by worldly wisdom.

Memory lingers on going with my uncles to harvest the maize, and pumpkins or potatoes. The potato and pumpkin paddocks were generally about two acres each to give room for ploughing with bullocks, and often as not a mile from the homestead. This would be partly to ensure safety from fowls, pigs or other domestic marauders; and the spot would be selected for its freedom from giant trees that had to be grubbed by hand, or it might be a fertile patch of alluvial soil. In earlier days one garden had been made across the creek. Its gooseberries and currants remained and we loved to get our horses and ride across to garner them. Pumpkins and maize grew in company with melons towards one end, and a row of giant sunflowers as decoration, as only enough seeds were saved for the succeeding season's crop. Sunflowers remain in memory as a father flower and are favourites. The potatoes were stored in the stable, which had its "end room" for the purpose. The pumpkins went in the hay, plenty for men and beasts and to give to neighbours in the highlands where they would not grow. Nothing ever rotted till well on in spring. There were no diseases in fruits or vegetables. Australia was as yet an uninfected and but slightly-infested heaven.

To such a harvest the men would take the bullock dray

and their lunches. I would be self-importantly assisting and you would think a nuisance to able-bodied young men who worked hard all day. But no, the surviving dearly-loved uncle at ninety still laughs about my company on one of these jaunts. When I got home Grandma inquired had I behaved myself. "Yes!"

"Did you say your grace before your victuals?"

"No."

"Why didn't you say grace?"

"I had nothing to say it on."

Grace before and after meals was never omitted. I said mine loudly and unctuously, I am sure, hands together in a Gothic arch and elbows on the table—the only time that elbows were permitted there. I never knew my mother to put her elbows on the table during meals, nor to sit with her knees crossed, nor to fidget or sprawl.

That particular episode must have taken place at this era, because I remember being on the diningroom table in the middle of the mail-bags, and I was too small previously to have been there. The mail filled all with zestful anticipation. The mailman on his weekly journey rarely arrived without bringing someone known or unknown, who needed hospitality for a night or longer. On this occasion he brought a gentleman with a loud laugh for his own wit, which I echoed with infant relish. Later I observed, "The Doctor does like to hear himself talk!" which was so obviously a repetition as to embarrass all but me.

A great-uncle, dictatorial, opinionated and argumentative, collided with me when I was again among the mail-bags. I made some puncturing remark about him, no doubt relished, for Uncle was not a favourite with his nephews no matter how charmingly his nieces deferred to him. His temper was short and arrogant. Someone apologized for my precocity while secretly enjoying it.

Uncle observed, "There is nothing more obnoxious than

27

a precocious child, especially a girl. One thing to be thankful for is that such abortions always die young." He predicted an early end for me, which would be a relief to everyone. No doubt he was justified in his irritation but the prophecy was not fulfilled.

The sequel is that as the last of his tribe, he returned to visit my mother, a favourite with all the clan. At the age of eighty-three he crossed the continent from Adelaide to Melbourne on a motor-cycle. There some fool with a dray ran into the machine in a side street and disabled it so that he had to finish the journey to Sydney by train. My heart warmed to the hardy, eccentric old individualist, rigorously gentlemanly in personal habits despite age and disabilities. I was the one most interested in and tolerant of his eccentricities; and, as he was almost stone deaf and I the only one who could make him hear, my heresies could not sour our association. We were a comfort and pleasure to each other and apparently he had no recollection of his early prophecy.

Half-a-dozen great-nieces and nephews rallied to give him an honoured and affectionate home-coming. The younger ones considered it was a lesson in style to see him unfurl his table-napkin, and regarded him as a distinguished museum piece. They liked too the way his well-tended beard shone like silver, and his deafness allowed their mischievous sense of humour and gay ribaldries regarding his peculiarities and pronounced character to seem joyous high spirits, which indeed they were.

7

Driving the bullocks

IT is not quite clear in my mind which incidents preceded which in some of those divided between Bobilla and Ajinby. I was still tiny and at Bobilla when some clash with discipline upset me. A habit of brushing so that I muddied my white stockings above my boot tops gave Mary extra trouble. To cure me, Mother set me to wash my own stockings. I was puddling in a little bucket when the kind-hearted Charlie came by on some errand, probably to get a glimpse of Mary.

"Cheer up!" said he. "I'll give you a rub."

"No," said Mother. "Charlie has his work and you have yours. You must learn to consider others."

This upset me, for I remember Mother chanting,

> "For aye she loot the tears down fall
> For Jock o' Hazledean."

Uncle Hil appeared and again eased the situation by inviting me to drive the bullocks.

Station bullocks were the aristocrats of their profession. Their lives were hard now and again if a bout of fencing were on and they had to drag logs by rough tracks, and they had several tough trips yearly for fifty miles forth and back again to one of the townships for supplies: but they were not driven to time on poor rations on boggy roads and beaten over lean ribs till they coughed piteously like some of the unfortunates in the carrying trade.

The bull is a synonym for madness, but the ox is the wisest and gentlest, the most dignified, and one of the most useful of domestic workers. He could be put to the plough, or packed where drays could not go, had a repertory in haulage, and finally and barbarously could be eaten. A trained bullock is even more sensible than a cow for he is free from a cow's temperamental and maternal fantods. Our bullocks suffered from sore feet on flinty tracks, and their briskets and shoulders must often have been painful when fresh to the crude and cruel yokes and bows. Uncle Hil grieved for their suffering in holding loads till they were forced to their knees and in danger of choking. There were other long weeks when they fed or dozed and chewed their cud in the choicest river paddocks without disturbance.

Ours were shorthorns, big handsome creatures of various markings. Their hides ranged from pure white to dark red or a darker brindle, or spotted. The most handsome were the strawberry roans, "a cattle carpet roan and red".

The bullocky has passed into legend and folk story as one of the most colourful of early pioneers. He was a hard doer for a hard job, a fierce individualist, and the boss himself was not always successful in altercations with him. He lived on the roads under the waggon or dray, in flood or drought, in heat or cold, alone, hardy and rough. His language was impious and vituperative and of such potency that legend has it that an artist of the species once swore and flayed the rails of a fence into a living team of bullocks. On the big stations of the wealthy squatters the bullocky engaged in haulage all the year round; sometimes there were two of the vocation and their off-siders. In the smaller holdings where the owners did most of the work with but few paid hands, all the men could handle bullocks just as they could all ride and shoot and fence and use axe and saw to build a home.

On Bobilla Uncle Hil was the master in training and using bullocks. It was akin, perhaps, to his understanding of children. He had the gentleness, the patience and the sympathy, and was esteemed for his skill in this department, as my father's second brother was admired as a whip.

"Come on, don't cry, or you won't be able to see which way the bullocks go."

The big beasts stood in the shade of the sally-trees at the back of the kitchen, philosophically chewing their cud and dribbling. They were yoked to a pole-chain with a hauling chain and its hook straight in the path behind them. They towered above me big as elephants.

"Now off you go! Let me see how well you can do it." I must have the long-handled whip with its big belly and long fall and lash. Uncle Hil placed it upright in my hands. Its weight toppled me over backwards. Uncle Hil saved me from shame by laughing with me, not at me, as he stood me right end up and balanced the handle with a finger while I clung to it on my own level.

"They won't need the whip. We'll just carry it."

I yelled in confident imitation, "Gee off, Strawberry! Come up, Snowy!"

Uncle Hil was silent. Words are superfluous with bullocks and horses. They are telepathic. The beautiful harmonious creatures moved smoothly as one.

It was a stupendous moment. The satisfaction and wonder of obedience from those big forms remains with me yet. The first exercise of power. We walked at a leisurely pace through the main gate to circle the orchard and come in at the back gate past the hayshed and the water track, and stopped where we started. This enlarged into one of the occasions when Uncle Hil took me home with him to Aunt Ignez. They lived a few miles distant.

Aunt Ignez was not rated as the beauty of her family nor considered remarkably clever by Mother and Aunt A. but those two young women were without exaggeration transcendent in resourcefulness and skill so that it was hard on competitors. Aunt Ignez suffered from violent and prolonged flatulence and was often irascible. Probably she was the victim of what today is coddled and relieved as a duodenal ulcer. She could have contracted one when living on the hard restricted diet of the earliest days at Bobill with her brothers when it was very wild and inaccessible. A mountain peak there is named in her honour.

"How is Ignez these days?" inquired Mother.

"She'd be all right if it wasn't for the wind. I don't know what to do for it. Gosh! that unfortunate woman has enough wind to start the bagpipes."

This led to acquaintance with three maladies of old ladies, who had to imbibe concoctions to break the wind or cut the phlegm, or bring up the bile.

I cannot envision any more saturating indulgence than was mine during my sojourns with that pair while they awaited their own family. Uncle would put me on his pommel at the end of day. I recall every contour of the way. The swift clear streams under us as we crossed were a thrill, especially the two crossings of the river, sometime to the girths, with the shod hoofs cracking loudly on its boulders. I babbled all the way and Uncle Hil conversed as to an equal.

There were differences in Aunt Ignez's flower garden. Today my own contains a *genista fraganta* in memory of the hedge of this, my introduction to such an ornament. The shrubs were pruned to the height of Uncle Hil's shoulder, after which they bushed out and were cut like a square box above the fence top. Barney, a pet ram, was hut away during my visits lest he should butt me. Barney did not like me, I am sure.

I was made the centre of attention, never a moment lacked its enfolding gratification. Aunt Ignez even sat me on the diningroom table so I could be with her while she sewed or crocheted, a licence never permitted by Mother. She made me dillybags of bright prints with a drawing-string and decorated with whorls of herringbone braid, which Mother and Aunt A. considered primitive efforts, but to me they were untold treasures. Uncle Hil managed to procure exhilarating presents such as a little black box of papier-maché with Chinese figures in gold, the inner rim of which was eaten in parts by some brown butterflies which I forgot for a fortnight, but which were able to fly away when released.

Aunt Ignez let me sit up a little later at nights—always the desire of a child—until she would sweep me into her arms and take me off to bed, laughingly exclaiming, "Oh, you're too much of a pet! We'll make an oddity of you if we are not careful."

They kept me with them during the night in a bed of my own, a kind of large cradle which Uncle Hil had made, and called a crib. Children must have been extravagantly prized as guests in those quieter days, otherwise there was no need for elders to have fashed themselves with me. I had a reputation as an amusing chatterbox, and I would set off with anyone I liked anywhere, agog for travel. At night I did not collapse into sobs and fret for my mother. To undress and go to bed with a new set of elders with a slightly different routine was adventure. I had no fear of elders, no matter how fierce their beards or loud their voices, so long as people did not wake in me swift instinct-ive dislike. This could be embarrassing with a child so naguily articulate. An old sea captain once asked me for a kiss. I refused.

"Why won't the little girl give me a kiss?"

"Because I don't like you."

"And why don't you like me?"

"Because you are a nasty old man and smell of rum."

It would be difficult for my parents to rebuke me. They were strict against deceit or saying behind people's back what we could not say to their faces. Father would maintain that a child could not be punished for speaking the truth. Life at large would soon chasten it for such foolishness.

"What a dear friendly little girl!" I recall on another occasion.

"Much too friendly," commented Mother. "Come away. You mustn't be a nuisance."

An elderly fossicker had brought his wife with him to the gullies and she had come to the homestead for mail, etc. Women were precious visitants because so rare. She must have impressed me as a grandmother. I wanted to climb on to her lap. I missed Grandma's. My successor had banished me from Mother's. When she took me up I was disappointed. She was so stout that she had no lap. It was like trying to sit on a melon. I was puzzled that it should be so much less comfortable than men's, which were like top rails on which one could ride-a-cock-horse to Banbury Cross.

Years later I returned in time to see Aunt Ignez and Uncle Hil before they left this life, to which they contributed only good and from which at the end they had so little. Uncle Hil had two horticultural treasures to share with me. One was a perfumed flower, the small stars of which were velvet bejewelled when seen under the magnifying glass. Uncle and I took up positions on our hunkers as of old in adoration. The other was a peach-tree laden with the sweetest fruit, funny little peaches flat on one side. Aunt Ignez was pitifully frail and supposed to be losing her memory, but she had not forgotten me and had a present for me as of yore.

"Oh, dear, you're just as full of talk as when you were a child."

"Auntie, dear, I'm sorry. I always talk too much."

"No!" said she firmly. "There could never be too much of your talk. You were always a brave and clever little girl, and you haven't changed."

I thank her for her generous "brave"—it comforts me, who am *not* brave.

8

Getting sophistication

A LONG hard journey by bridle track across some o
the highest ranges in Australia lay between Bobill
and Ajinby and Gool Gool, my grandmother's town. Suc
expeditions were not lightly taken by Mother but visit
would be made at intervals for births, weddings or funeral
Funerals were the rarest of the three in a tribe mostly o
young people with robust elders vigorously engaged i
longevity. On all occasions when my mother was of th
party I went as a matter of course. One exception therefor
remains in my mind.

The house was left in charge of Mrs M'G., the wife o
the horse-breaker, who came for the purpose from her hu
three miles away with her two infants, one of my age
Mother instructed me to be obedient and keep out of mis
chief. She provided a little book in which were written m
name and that of Ethel M'G. If either were naughty a ba
mark was to be put against her name.

Ethel was more worldly-wise than I. She had had th
sophistication of association with miscellaneous childre
when her mother returned at intervals to help her forme

mistress. The mother had been, before marriage, a parlour-maid at one of the big stations forty miles away. Ethel and her sister were given to violent tantrums never before witnessed by me. They were lively entertainment, to be compared with the frenzy of a pup when first introduced to a collar and chain.

We played at riding with slips from gum saplings for horses. Girls ran beside, boys bestrode their steeds. Ethel was fat and slow and resented my speed. Every chance she got she trod on the tail of my horse. I asked Mrs M'G. to give her a bad mark. She was deaf to my allegations so I returned to galloping round the orchard. It had not entered my head to obstruct a play horse any more than it would to try such dangerous tricks with real animals, but now I decided to do as Ethel did. I slowed for her to lumber ahead, well-pleased with herself, and then jumped on her horse's tail. She ran bawling to her mother. A mark against me was promptly logged. I again explained volubly that Ethel had many times done this to me and at last I had retaliated merely to teach her.

"She has bad manners, you should teach her."

Mrs M'G. remained obtuse. When Mother came home there were pages of marks against me and none against Ethel.

This was more astounding than wounding to me, even when Mother in receiving the report remarked, "I knew my lady would be the ringleader."

I was not hurt by the injustice. Anything of the nature was so new that it did not penetrate. My mind was exercised by the stupidity of Mrs M'G., a grown-up, about what had really happened. My parents never similarly failed in discernment. I dismissed Mrs M'G. as rabble, which was natural at the age when one's own parents know more than anyone else in the world, and have the only correct way of doing all things.

37

In the wider world later Mrs M'G.'s a-moral bias was so common as to be normal. I discussed the difference in my own parents' attitude with a charming old friend of the remittance variety who was spending a month or a year with us when I had reached teens.

"Parents come in two kinds," said he, "those who think their obnoxious brats can do no wrong because they are their own and act like it, and those who are equally certain the other way around. Mine jolly-well never left me in doubt as to the group they were in. It was the stick for me without my depositions being taken if anyone laid a complaint about me."

As I grew older I sometimes offended polemically with subversive notions, even about the Deity, but my tendencies were never of an evil or perverted nature. I was obedient physically. If forbidden to touch anything, or warned not to stray outside the garden, to disobey never occurred to me. This was of some comfort to my elders. The result to me was that I enjoyed liberty of movement free from constant supervision. In some ways I was not so advanced as other children of my age. It was only in curiosity and ideas that I exceeded limits. Give me a book or toy and it would be well preserved. This was due to my mother's training and my own finickiness. Her sewing-machine is still capable of beautiful work. Her books remained firm in their bindings, unspotted or unmarked in their pages. To dog-ear a book or lick a finger to turn a page was disgusting to her.

Another experience was combined with something like Ethel's behaviour shortly afterwards. A visiting cousin and I were each given two tiny candy slippers and adjured to try who could keep hers the longest. The cousin's disappeared the same day. Mine would have remained untouched till they disintegrated if the cousin had not found them a week later; and, when I saw her, only the heel of one slipper remained. The loss of the treasure and the banditry revolted me less than such a lack of self-control, only I did not know what it was at the time.

Where I must have been a trial was in insatiable curiosity concerning all action around me, coupled with exceptional powers of seeing, hearing, remembering and reporting; and I could not be shushed or argued or bamboozled out of my findings. I lacked the overplussed imagination by which some children conjure up a world of their own or fabricate happenings so beyond actuality, so far from truth on prosaic levels, that they enjoy the licence of habitual criminals. No credence is given them. Their parents take refuge in the theory, "They'll grow out of it."

I was so accurate that I could be consulted as an oracle to settle doubtful points. On the other hand this was a menace because I could not be discounted when I saw or heard that which denied to my victims their decent reticences and subterfuges. An example on each side of the ledger. Charlie (one of the rouseabouts) and the domestic helper loathed me when I hid under the kitchen table—I sat there for no known reason that I can summon, except the satisfaction of being where no one suspected. The man was sitting on the stool beside the wall, and had the girl's hand in his. I retailed what I heard and no doubt it was quite innocent. What held me was that Charlie's dark face, not usually given to merriment, was aglow and pleading, and that Mary, a thumping extrovert Susan Nipper, always being chiacked by the men and able to hold her own, was standing somnolently without motion or sound listening to the old old story. These poor dears were helpless against me, for my mother held that it was not wise to draw attention by reprimand to what should be forgotten in a child's mind—let it fade.

It was another pair of sleeves when I was under the same table when a dashing cousin of Mother's after a hard day's riding was having an early meal to stay his hunger. He was talking at the top of his ego, which was lively and assertive. Suddenly he insisted that one of the pups had got in. No dog was allowed inside the house. When no pup appeared following his threats, he investigated. I was discovered. He was a young man with a red beard and known for his quick temper. His threats were violent and abusive.

"Beastly nipper! She's a pest! Ought to be choked! Only dogs get under tables, and dogs are kicked outside, where they belong. Better be careful! That's what'll happen to you. You'll be kicked clean out through the back gate in mistake before you know what's happened to you. And serve you right!"

Neither Mary nor the cousin had a spark of love for me.

I don't know why I liked to get under a table—any table. I can remember the bumps I got on my head before I could gauge when to stand upright when coming out.

The other example was with the Commissioner for Crown Lands. He had the power to reassess the value of the runs which were held from the Crown, a gentleman to court and for whom the "end room" wore its best linen and the dining-table quite a Christmas of good viands. As he sat by the fire after a day's inspection he was interested in the number of times one of the streams had been crossed and re-crossed.

"It wriggles like a snake. Have you any idea, F . . . , how many times we crossed it?"

Father said he was so used to that route that he had forgotten the count. I piped up, "Seven times."

"Dear me," said the gentleman, surprised, for I had been on my best behaviour and not ordinarily intrusive; but this was beyond suppression. "How do you know, little girl?"

"Because I counted."

I had lately been taught to count to twenty, and exercised my knowledge to the utmost.

"What a remarkably clever little girl!" He gave me more attention than was considered good for any robustious ego for the remainder of his stay, and remains as a charming figure.

In departing he said, "I think you are going to be an author. Goodbye, clever little girl! Remember my prophecy and don't forget to send me a copy of your first book."

9

Social appearances

ONE of the trips to visit relatives at Gool Gool before I was five is clear in recollection for the social blunders I made. Mother and I stayed at the home of Mother's Uncle William (my great-uncle) and Aunt Lizzie.

In Aunt's garden I saw for the first time a border of striped ribbon grass. There was another of pansies which filled me with greedy desire, but my training was such that they were safe from molestation. The ribbon grass did not seem to be a flower, so I plucked a leaf. It was silky and pliable. I picked more and returned to view with my booty. I never had any need to be sly or to hide anything from my elders.

"Naughty little puss! To meddle with the flowers in Auntie's garden! You must *never* touch other people's things."

Aunt Lizzie gently intervened, but Mother maintained that character and desirable habits must be inculcated early.

"Promise me that you'll never touch a flower in anyone's garden without permission."

I promised so deeply that I still cannot take flowers from other people's gardens with full ease, even when made free of them. Mother was deep in the toilet of the baby in arms. Aunt Lizzie called softly from outside the doorway. She took me by the hand and led me to the ribbon grass and pansies.

"Look at my pansies! Don't you think they are prettier than ribbon grass?"

I doted. Pansies are my delight.

"They are waiting to be picked, all of them! One bunch for your mother and the other for you and me together."

I was spell-bound. Intoxicated. Oh, child delight! Oh, sweet Aunt Lizzie!

On Sunday Aunt Lizzie's two little grand-daughters called to escort me to Sundayschool. The elder, E., all her life has been outstanding. Her charm and ability were with her from childhood. She was in charge of the two juniors. Everyone trusted her. That hot November day we walked in the soft dust of the rich soil through lanes rife with English hedge roses—climbers almost as lovely as the banksia vine at Ajinby, but the clusters of bloom instead of pale gold were pink and white, and perfumed, superior to the scentless Dorothy Perkins of later fashion. We went by the river famous for its beauty with its weeping willows—surely the biggest in the world—and with some towering Lombardy poplars and the roses, descendants of originals set by members of my tribe.

It was my only appearance in Sundayschool anywhere. My recollection of the procedure is vague. The teacher early conducted me to the entrance porch and told me to stay there till E. came to take me home. I accepted this without suspicion of derogation. I had company in Willie, a boy older and bigger. He was not very responsive to my friendly chatter. He was restless and kept running outside and in again and climbing up on the back of the seat, which was to me purposeless and close to flouting the rules in whatever game we were engaged.

A grown-up cousin of Mother's was there when we returned. She gave me charming attention. I had much to communicate about the peculiarities of Willie.

"His clothes were torn and dirty, and he had a nasty smell. I didn't like him." My olfactory nerve matched my long sight and acute sense of hearing.

"He wanted me to run outside with him, but the teacher said we had to stay there till she came back."

The elegant young lady said it was not nice that I should be put outside with a boy like Willie.

"He had bad manners. His mother ought to have taught him how to behave."

E. may have explained. I have no recollection of rebuke or shame for misbehaviour. No one mentioned the matter again. It remained to be dug out long after. No doubt I had taken charge of the congregation and the teacher had had to take measures to survive.

The Sundayschool picnic took place next day and the able and valiant E. again escorted me. Each child had to take its own drinking vessel. Aunt Lizzie produced a little tot for me. Mother charged me not to lose it. E. was as precocious as I, and had associated with other children in various groups, which had trained her to be a dependable member of society and a comfort to everyone. My segregation with and imitation of my elders made of me a nonpareil that was a liability.

The picnic feast was my first experience of long tables in the open under the blossoming acacia trees that dotted the park-like church domain. I was dazed by the piles of cakes, but had no idea of plunging in uninvited. There was still nothing on my plate when all the choicest varieties had been gobbled. One of the elders in charge, noting this, fobbed me off with a bun. Yah! It looked so big and gay,

nd was mere bran after the rich cakes I had been used to.
Therewith began my contempt for and repudiation of buns
s *ersatz.*

I was captivated by the masses of cut flowers that beauti-
ed the long tables. Bowls and bowls of tea roses—the
Cloth of Gold, the Maréchal Ney, La France, the Maiden's
Blush—and maidenhair fern from the banks of the river,
whose song was cool and soothing where we sat. The
memory of my mother town is inseparable from the scent
of roses, overpowering as they wilted in the heat.

After the feast I was too small and untrained to join in
the games, and shrank from their roughness. Rebuffed and
unadaptable, I got separated from the others. That did not
distress me. I carried my entertainment within. My preoccupation was to obtain a spray of the acacia bloom, a
new flower and perfume. I clutched my tot, a direct
charge, and wandered away to seek a tree with a bough
within reach.

It was time to go home. E. became worried to find me.
She had forgotten me in the games. I came to view as the
groups dispersed. A bigger, shaggier girl ran to me and
demanded my tot, saying "It's mine! You took it from me."
I firmly contradicted this, marvelling at her stupidity to
claim something that had never left my hand.

"Teacher sent me to get it and wash it. You can't take it
home dirty."

This was plausible. She grabbed the tot and ran off dis-
regarding my assertion that it was bad manners to snatch
things. She was as uncongenial as Willie to me. I never saw
the tot nor that bigger, bolder girl again. She was so much
older than I, so much more astute in business, that I wonder
what she achieved in life.

E. was distressed that I had lost the tot. "I didn't lose it.
A big girl took it away to be washed."

"What girl?"

"A big girl. She didn't have pretty clothes. She had ba[d] manners. I didn't like her."

The teacher said it could not be helped, and told E. [to] take me home. She explained to her grandmother, "S[he] didn't lose the tot. A big girl grabbed it."

"She had bad manners, she snatched it. Her mother ough[t] to have taught her it's bad manners to snatch things."

"Silly child, I told you to take care of it. You must go [to] town tomorrow to buy Auntie a new tot."

Aunt Lizzie again intervened softly. It seemed that s[o] many tots lay about the place that the removal of one w[as] a help. To console me for the loss she presented me wi[th] one of the wonders of the world, a tiny parasol whic[h] fitted me and which opened and furled like my mother'[s]

Mother had brought the nursemaid so that she too cou[ld] enjoy a holiday with her family, and was without her hel[p] on the following afternoon when she set out to pay a vi[sit] on foot about half a mile distant. Mother carried the bab[y] and I was to take its extras. Ordinarily this would hav[e] inflated me with self-importance. That day was devoted [to] the parasol with the tenacity of the boy on the burnin[g] deck. Both hands were required, to hold it tightly on m[y] sunbonnet, eyes upturned. Mother was trebly burdened b[y] the heat, the fat infant—no cuddle seats then—and h[er] inability to get me moving at more than a snail's pac[e] while I concentrated on the parasol. This happening w[as] preserved in Mother's exasperation and she would recou[nt] it as a warning against presents of parasols to children.

10

Death

DEATH came once to that new home at Bobilla during our occupancy, to the youngest inmate. My baby sister died before her first year.

The tiny coffin, tenderly carpentered by the men about the place, was covered with white satin. To me the baby seemed to be asleep as I had so often seen her. The waxen face was of unearthly beauty and promised the perfection of another sister's. The white-robed figure was surrounded by violets, snowdrops and daffodils. They were the only daffodils of their kind I have seen in Australia. I have seen their like only once again, in London, when a friend sent me a box of "daffs" and wild violets from the woods in the Midlands.

I can see Mother, comforted by Aunts A. and Ignez, with tears on her cheeks, gently falling, no storming or loss of control. It was one of the few times in all her long life of cruel bereavements that I saw her give way to tears. I never saw my father or any other Australian adult man weep. Thus I grew to eschew tears, though after one or two desolating blows they have come to my relief.

I was told by my father that I must not go with the men, a rare exclusion from station doings. I followed at a distance unnoticed. No one looked around to see me. It seemed to me quite a company of men. Everyone available would have come to show sympathy for my mother and to be "mates" with my father . . . everyone of that company except myself, now dead.

I don't remember any of the turmoil and anxiety that must have preceded the death of the infant nor of feeling any grief for her loss. It remains however in my consciousness as a solemn occasion; I recall my indignation, when the burial was completed, to see Charlie, who was carrying the spade, and one of his cronies laughing together about their own youthful concerns as they came up the hill. Grief for an infant's demise is entirely a woman's unless the deceased is bound up with property or male pride in self-perpetuation.

Father enclosed a plot with sturdy corner posts and durable palings of mountain-ash, all carefully dressed and fired as a precaution against devouring insects. My mother planted an elm-tree as a monument. I saw it some years later, a glorious young sentinel over the corner posts, still standing. Later again there was nothing but the elm-tree in the pasturage. Today that mark has been obliterated by fires, and the plot is one of the uncounted bush graves as unmarked as that of Moses in Moab.

11

Gardening

AN English elm my mother set at Ajinby was for long a
noble landmark after the family left the old home.
s capacity for throwing dense shade and holding-off a
ower made it the refuge of travellers until it was mutil-
ed by a sub-species, known as tourists, moronic and a-
cial, which lighted campfires under it. Mother grew an-
her at Bobilla, which early provided shade beyond the
ower of our eucalypts, and the first hop leaves were the
light of us children. The space around it was sown with
grass known as Italian rye and kept short by the scythe.
'e were proud of the tree and the park-like air it lent,
led by the indigenous sally-gums spared for their sym-
etry.

Tall old elms with feathered trunks, resembling those to
seen in the hedgerows between fields in Devonshire
rms, guard (or did till recently) the stonewalled garden
here Mother was born. They must have been as dear in
r memory as the trees of Ajinby are in mine.

There were no lawns in my childhood. Mother would
ve revelled in the green velvet surfaces, smooth from

close-shaving and a hundred years of the roller, that beauify England. She did her best with the Italian grass and th
scythe. In the centre of her flower garden she had a sizeable round plot thus sown and kept in order. In this sh
set daffodils in some fashion she must have seen in pictur
or been told of by her English grandfather. It was thes
bulbs that supplied the blooms for the dead baby. The
had short stems and round fat heads of tight-packed petal
No other daffodils impress me, no matter how big the
single cups, nor how trumpeted by idolators. I thing of m
mother's daffodils as sisters to Emily Dickinson's flow
which also was chubby, and untied "her yellow bonn
beside the village door".

I was born into a tribe of inveterate gardeners. Whe
my maternal great-grandfather added farming to grazir
he had the aid of a gardener trained on one of the duc
estates in England whom he had lured from a crowd bour
for the diggings. This man became an identity as "old N
Calloway" and trained three generations of both sex
to sow and prune and set both gardens and orchards. H
misplacement of words remains in one example:

"Mr Calloway, what course would you take with a te
ant who refuses to vacate the premises?"

"I'd give him a written injection.'

My mother's generation, regardless of sex, could pru
and graft and bud orchard trees as a matter of cours
Tremendous labour by my father went to the making
Mother's garden where so lately the towering primordi
trees had reigned. In each corner at the end farthest fro
the house were two clumps of rasping pampas grass, t
glory of which were the plumes of white fluff that the
renewed each year like the crests of the knights in effig
who ride in the Tower of London. All around the fen
were monthly roses, rarely without a bloom even on t
austere highlands. Between the knights' plumes was a bo

er of the lilies of France, half of purple, half of white. Near the house was a luxuriant border of Sweet William, richly perfumed. There was a gate at either side, one with frame to support an arch of English honeysuckle. Its mild perfume hardly compensated for its straggling and inconspicuous flowers, but the bees and we children liked the honey in them. Near by was a lilac-tree with glorious blossoms and a perfume of paradise never to be forgotten, never to be confused with any other. As a companion it had a *rosa weigela*. At the other gate was a laburnum that cascaded in a glory of gold.

Here also Mother had a novelty in two hop vines. Father erected two very tall poles for them to form a striking arch. I never saw any of these plants elsewhere till they were pointed out to me from the train on the way to Canterbury, Kent. They later provided me with an instance of the tenacity and surety of knowledge early ingrained. One afternoon a party from the Victoria League was being entertained by a visit to the river gardens of famous residences on the Thames at Richmond. We were belated and our guide missed the way to the house where we were awaited. As we ran about, the light of a match showed the outline of a vine on a summerhouse. Someone exclaimed about the beauty of the silhouetted grape leaves.

"Hops," I corrected as I came in contact with them.

In the drawingroom this guest again mentioned the beauty of the grape leaves. "As a matter of fact they are hops," said the hostess.

"How did you know that in the dark?" someone inquired of me. "Do you have hop fields in Australia?"

Our hostess responded, "I'm always astonished by the affection New Zealanders and Australians have for ferns and how they know them by touch. It must be the same with grape or hop leaves."

Many of the English garden flowers that could endure

frost flourished in the virgin soil. Mother's garden was preserve for emigrants stoutly fenced in from wild Aus tralians. A native violet persistently resisted extirpation The blossoms, large and on firmer stalks than the importe varieties, with petals distinctly veined and as though cu from slightly thicker material, had a tinge of cyclamen t redden the purple. The seed pods were exactly the same a the English variety. At a glance the flowers could not hav been distinguished from the others, but they had no per fume and the leaves were longer, narrower and indente more like a pansy's. They were safe from horses, whic would crop the English variety to the ground. Like othe native plants they resisted alike extermination and trans plantation. This clump was on a path where Mother per mitted no intrusions. It was constantly removed to one c the beds, where it never struck but would reappear on th path from some thread of root as hardily as a dock c dandelion.

Mother early introduced me to the delights of gardenin by giving me a little part of my own to tend and kee clear of weeds. It is well to root familiarly in the earth and Bobilla's was unpolluted, a-septic. I had served a fir apprenticeship to mud pies. In small cleared spaces the ster frosts raised icicles like splinters of glass. When melted b the sun the clay underneath had a consistency suitable fc modelling into pies and other shapes. I was first given packet of balsam seeds. Dear beautiful balsams, amenabl to grow in pots and quickly blooming for impatient chile hood. Next I had a yellow pansy with a dark face to ten I was an assiduous and obedient pupil and as a reward wa to have a flower of my very own, different from any othe

Mother brought out the seed catalogue, one of thos magical magazines which after half an hour's browsin leave one in an Eden of burgeoning flowers, vegetabl and fruit. Away went the order on pack-horse by bridl rack through gullies and streams and mountain gaps to ome mysterious other world. Mother's choice was an outized bulb. She showed me how to set it.

"You must water it in moderation and keep the weeds way, and leave it *alone*—entirely alone. Never touch the round near it. It knows what to do itself. It won't grow f you meddle with it."

"Mother, what is it going to be like?"

"I can't quite describe. We haven't another flower to ompare it with."

"What is it called?"

"A tulip."

To see the first leaves of plants or seedlings break from he earth is an entrancement that never stales. I used to t and watch for the tulip's appearance like a cat near a nouse hole. But the Dutch emigrant was tardy.

Spring was near. Grandpa arrived to divert my attention. The horse muster was imminent and Grandpa still liked to e in it, if only thereby. His two elder sons said he was etting childish but his ageless wisdom was increasing and ny father had great reverence for him. He was respected y all the youths and outsiders as "the old Gentleman". He ad a resounding voice and an Irish brogue. It was claimed hat he could be heard for miles out on the runs as he eproved the dogs or exhorted the ignorant colonials. He eplored their lack of conversational powers and that they ut the fat off their cooked meat and flung to the dogs vhat Grandpa considered dainties but which they called ffal. In any case the dogs had to be fed and the head of beast, the liver and other bovine giblets were containers or strychnine for dingoes.

Grandpa was audible otherwise. He inhabited the end oom and his pitiful limp resounded on the boards of the eranda. He had too a definite odour of strong plug to-acco, which he smoked all the time and sometimes enhanced by a toddy of rum. Till well over sixty, despite a dislocated hip, he still cut-out at the musters on a dependable and clever horse named Blocky.

Grandpa was a rabid gardener in the vegetable domain. The sexes were separated in gardening. Men were proud of their women's gardens and did the heavy work for them but would have considered it effeminate themselves to potter with flowers. Indeed, they had little time in the ceaseless struggle to make homes in the bush, but a plot of vegetables was important where each had to grow his own or live by beef and bread alone.

The usual acres had been logged-in at a distance for potatoes, pumpkins, etc. We had another garden for the softer, smaller vegetables. It was at the foot of a knoll at the back of the premises where the soil was alluvial. It was enclosed by saplings set closely and deeply like a stockade against burrowing native animals. The rabbits had not then arrived. The soil was fertile and loaded with restoring animal dung. To water it a race had been cut for a quarter of a mile or so from the river. Much labour for one or two pairs of hands at the week-ends. Set around the fence were gooseberry bushes and red and white currant and raspberry canes, which throve in that latitude, but never quite reached the standard of those met later in England. Then there were rows of all the ordinary vegetables.

My father imparted to me his own wonder at the potency of seeds.

"Think how clever the little seeds are. See these, they look almost alike, but put them in the earth and one will bring up a turnip and the other a radish. One tiny seed not as big as a pin's head is so brave and clever it can be put in the ground all by itself and will bring up a great big cabbage you couldn't lift."

When he grew old and had leisure, gardening became a passion with him. He had the industry and patience of a

54

Chinese gardener and such tenderness that no care irked him. Were there a garden hereafter, all the little plants therein would troop towards the entry to welcome him. When he was very old to see him set a fruit-tree or a rose-bush was a privilege. No haste, no skimping, no failures.

In the vegetable garden the youngsters were given rows of their own where they were free to follow their fancy as there was a super-abundance of seeds and soil. But the weeds were equally hearty and soon hid from view the small plants. Here Grandpa and descendants disagreed in procedure. When Grandpa found a sea of weeds he dug everything out then picked out the vegetables to replant in the clean space. Stooping to weed was beyond his dislocated hip: to dig at all with such lameness was a triumph of mind.

A theory was prevalent that root vegetables could not be transplanted with success. This has long been discredited by the parcels of beets, onions, etc. to be purchased at seed stores. Grandpa's wisdom or knowledge was ahead of local practice. The children clamoured for an edict against Grandpa for taking young parsnips and carrots out by the roots, which had been forbidden to them.

"Well," said Father mildly, "no one must interfere with Grandpa's gardening. Grandpa knew everything before any of us was born. You must do what you are told, but Grandpa can do what he likes. Is that clearly understood?"

It was. Father used an apothegm as an apology for his ever-failing clemency towards nearly all errors short of capital crimes. To Grandpa he said, "Let the children potter along and learn by experience. There is plenty of room and plants for them to prove both theories. 'Live and let live.'"

"Moi, oh, moi!" said Grandpa.

12

The tulip

THESE activities took my mind from the tulip, but on day it was found to have put forth thick green leaves. watered it, plucked out any weed, watched it once mor like a cat at a mouse hole. Again it seemed to be smitter by arrested development.

Mother was teaching me my alphabet and figures in preparation for education by a tutor among my cousins a the head station. First came light up-strokes and heavy down-strokes. Then pothooks and hangers and thus t letters and figures.

I was set to make the alphabet and letters from memory The curves of the figure three eluded my feeble fingers nor could I gauge the little pothook near the top of long down-stroke to compile *p*.

There was a lull in vegetable growing. In his leisur Grandpa read the newspapers interminably, but I had neve seen him writing. He would command, "Maurice, take th pen and write to So-and-So."

"Grandpa, you can read, can't you?"

"Sure, child, that's what I'm doing now." He laughed

Brilliant possibility! "Grandpa, can you write too?"

"Can I write! Moi, oh, moi! Can I write?" chortled Grandpa. "Can *you*? What is it you want me to do?"

"Grandpa, can you make a three?" I presented my slate. Grandpa could, and did. "Moi, oh, moi!"

"Grandpa, can you write a *p*?"

"Sure I can. I can eat one too. If we keep the garden watered and the weeds plucked away, we'll soon have peas galore."

Grandpa complied with ready good-will and no inquiries about rules and regulations. What a find! What an ally!

Grandpa and I had a secret. We looked at each other in the light of it. His eyes twinkled. Life was suddenly enriched and enlarged. He was ever ready to cheer and help me, ever sure that I was a remarkable specimen. He was a dear old man who asked little from life and got less. He took what was given him without complaints and never asked concessions for his lameness or age.

With Grandpa added to the other elders to make life thrilling from daylight to dusk, my very own plant was forgotten. It got on with its job in privacy and one day when I was strolling around the path playing some inner-life game with myself there was the *Tulip*! Something wonderful, something new! It is the only one I remember to have seen in Australia; nowhere have I seen another exactly like it. The new soil, space and natural fertilizer may have helped. It stood on a noble stem nearly as tall as myself, a big dark reddish bell. Every member of the household gathered to behold and exclaim. Anyone who called during its reign was not allowed to miss it. No doubt other gardens were honoured by tulips but I knew only the family's and a few others, and some of them but rarely on fleeting visits.

Uncle Hil's response was breathlessly awaited. In his deep comforting bass, it was perfect.

13

Bogeys and banshees banished

AN elderly friend lately confessed that he has alway
been terrified of the dark. Incredible! Such fear mus
have been inculcated during infancy.

Turkey chicks, calves and other nurslings are not bor
with fear. The tiny tortoises in the streams in Connecticu
do not slip off the rocks with their elders as a boat ap
proaches them. Children have no sense of danger. I ow
immunity from certain phobias to the attitudes and precept
of my parents. I love the night.

Father had been left much alone in the great bush fron
an early age and accepted it as natural. I absorbed fron
him his own wonder in the quiet majesty of our nights, in
turn lit by the moon, quite dark or full-spangled and glitter
ing free from coastal haze; vast, high-vaulted, such as sail
ors and bushmen knew above unpopulated seas and lands
Father had a similar attitude towards the sunset: he woul
inspect it like a pageant even when he had retired to town
He retained his sense of wonder. Mother did not have it in
so exaggerated a degree. She was sane and practical, withou
eccentricity.

Attempts on the part of nursemaids to control us by fanciful tales or frightening threats would have been forbidden. Our little servant girls, mere children themselves, had been born in lonelier spots on the edges of the larger runs and none was afraid of the dark because we had all there was of it. On winter nights it was unbroken except for a few feet around homemade tallow candles or slush lamps, a large kerosene lamp or the imperial log fires before which one could read or sew or talk with one's elders in a glow of comfort and warmth, never to be forgotten, never to be equalled.

I was without fear of horses, cattle, dogs or men because of familiarity with them from birth onwards. Some things I was warned against as dangerous and my attitude to these in certain cases solidified into permanent revulsion or fear. Mother sternly forbade us to go near the river unaccompanied. It was swift and treacherous when in flood. There were many deep holes used for swimming by the men but we children paddled in the shallows with Mother. Her inability to swim was a strange gap in ability beyond the ordinary with tools and machinery. She would try perseveringly all her life, and surfed till nearly eighty, but never could manage to float in water.

Father had known the Murrumbidgee, the bigger river, from his boyhood and could dive deeply and swim powerfully. On Sunday mornings when I was tiny he would take me for a walk on his shoulder by the river; and, unable to resist, would strip and plunge in. It was unsafe to leave me on the bank so I was stripped too and taken pick-a-back as you can sometimes see a duckling on the parent's back. It was a great adventure with just a little strain in it. Sometimes I would sit on Father's back or his chest while he floated, but mostly I would be slung around his neck while he swam on his side, which is the best way of swimming without commotion. Or I would seek among the water-worn pebbles for the "drake stones" and he would skip them along the surface of a smooth pool.

It was a great day when I found I could float on the water, and my fear of it vanished. I was always pottering at my parents' heels. Father took me before him all day miles out on the run, sometimes to burn off. He taught me to keep on the safe side of flames so that in later years I have not panicked when hair or garments have caught alight.

One of few memories of pain in childhood is connected with fire. Mother always gave me a bit of pastry as a beginning in the culinary art. Her pastry, as everything she did, was first class. I can still see myself patting my piece and enjoying the imprint of the lines in my paw upon it. These sometimes would be dark from mud pies or other experiments. The pastry would be baked beside mother and my pleasure in accomplishment was warm. However I could never persuade anyone, not even the accommodating Uncle Hil, to more than pretend to taste it.

"You can give it to the puppies or hens. They'll love it."

I had a tiny saucepan made in the image of its elders. It was of iron lined with enamel, and big enough to have boiled one egg, only I have no memory of a single egg being boiled at a time. The saucepan was much admired for its perfection and may have been a scale model from some exhibition. One day I set it on the hearth with its colleagues before the fire that was cooking the dinner. I ran back from outside to see how my cooking was going and slipped on the hearth stones so that my hand went into the rosy furnace of hardwood coals. I can see myself stretched there. I grabbed the saucepan and ran shrieking to Mother who quickly rendered the most competent treatment of the period. It was not a serious burn but Mother's skill and knowledge could not save me from some pain.

Again, I was four and playing with a little boy at Ajinby

got me to help him in some machination in which he
ught a hammer onto one of my fingers. That is a much
re painful memory than the burn. Perhaps there was an
ment of boys' cruelty in it. It was the third finger of
left hand. The nail turned black. In time it grew off
a new pink one came underneath.

14

Fairies skipped

PANTOMIME as well as much of Shakespeare on t
boards, stories designed for juveniles, and fairytales, ne
to be imbibed before the age of ten to hold the affectio
in maturity. Thus I have a distaste for fairies—that is the
tiny people who infest flowers like caterpillars.

I did not come in contact with books containing the
till I was adult, when they irritated me as trash: and t
juvenile department of a bookshop is to me a nightmare
untidiness, with glaring volumes of miscellaneous shap
and sizes and callow contents. Mother dismissed fairies
unwholesome imaginings and guarded her infants' min
from the heavier kind of fantasy also because in her ow
childhood she had been harrowed by the sorrows and tri
of the children in them. Little Red Riding Hood eat
by a wolf: two babies dying in the woods, lost and cover
by leaves: Jack and the Beanstalk, with the gruesome sl
ting of the giants' stomachs—horror stories with starvi
match-girls and frozen children. We had no starvi
match-girls; a straying child called out the countryside f
a hundred miles to the rescue.

In packing to leave Bobilla a stack of booklets with light paper covers displaying gnomes, dwarfs, bears, mushrooms and other fauna and flora came to light on top a bookcase. These contributions to my famed greed for reading had been intercepted; but Mother, unable actually burn a thing so precious as a book, had allowed them to become the only "unnecessary accumulation to harbour dust and moths" in her house.

She approved *Mother Goose* and had a big volume with all illustrations. In the middle of winter mornings she would put me on her knee beside one of the glorious fires, take off my high boots and stockings and chafe my feet and legs, always like ice no matter how much I trotted. While she brought me back to comfort she would indulge me with "Pat-a-cake, Pat-a-cake, Baker's Man"; "Little Miss Muffet"; "The Old Lady who Lived in a Shoe"; "Dickery-Dickery-Dock"; "Tom Thumbkins"; "One, Two, Buckle my Shoe"; "Jack and Jill" and "The Crooked Sixpence" with their cumulative repetition so fascinating to infancy; and all the immortal host. ·

Mother never attempted to sing. Father entertained me with ditties, short scraps of which remain in my mind:

> Sally had a magpie that was very fond of talking,
> She plucked a feather from his tail
> Every time she went out walking.
> Soon old Mag's tail hadn't a feather upon it
> You had the pleasure of seeing them stuck
> All round Sally's bonnet.

Another concerned Massa and brushing away the blue-tailed fly, "so early in the morning, so early in the morning, fore the break o' day." Sometimes to company he also sang:

> It's a very sad thing as most of us know,
> That life's full of troubles
> Wherever you go.

You ask at a ball, a dance or two
With a pretty little girl
You think likes you.
She is so tired, you really can't tell,
Then off she walks with another young swell.
It's really very unpleasant, it's really very unpleasant,
It's really very unpleasant, but it can't be helped, you know

These efforts were limited in scale and monotonous
tune, which as I grew older I laid to musical shortcomings
in Father. A lifetime later his tunes and words are being
resuscitated plus a buzzing banjo but with similar monotony
and in no better voice by an "artist" who packs large
concert halls and is acclaimed as a star.

I never was told stories like the children of today and
early grew superior to gaudily apparelled books designed
to lure young minds, and despised pompous pretentious
ones for older dullards. Having had the privilege of friend-
ship with Mr and Mrs Cobden-Sanderson and one of Mr
Cobden-Sanderson's pupils in the United States, I am acquainted with treasures of the bookbinder's art but do not
covet covers however resplendent. At Grandma's the books
allowed me in addition to the Bible and prayerbook were
few until I grew to Dickens and Scott. Among early friends
were Aesops's *Fables*. The edges of the cover were bound
with lead, the leaves were yellow and spotted with rust,
the illustrations old-fashioned woodcuts, sober and black.
My loyalty to that old volume is such that to see the beloved fables done up with coloured modern illustrations is
an offence. An ancient school reader was a second treasure.
Mother knew its contents by heart and there is a vagrant
memory that it was also my grandmother's. I devoured it
without guidance and came to the release of ballads. "The
Dream of Eugene Aram"; "Young Edmund"; "The Phil-
osopher's Scales"; "The Inchcape Rock"; "Signs of Rain"
were a few that I committed to memory. I itched to recite

these wonders but no one was interested in such familiar stuff. Thus was happily skipped the infant routine of standing up to repeat some rhyme or other in a shrill painful squeak—though such blooding in infancy might have armoured me against subsequent annihilating stage fright.

Fairytales could not be entirely unknown among literate people even on a remote cattle station. "Little Red Riding Hood", "The Babes in the Wood", "Jack and the Beanstalk" and "The Ugly Duckling" grew familiar by osmosis. Signs are that if introduced early I could have become addicted to juvenile literature. Because. A day that remains sacred was dominated by a story-teller with a child's book.

Mother said I was an exceptionally healthy child and never refused my food and was not given to tantrums. On the day of precious memory I had undergone senna tea which Grandma was likely to impose for bad manners or "frowardness", or as the catechism, for my good. Uncle avers that she always chastised him in the morning as a duty got out of the way betimes like family prayers, etc., whether he had been naughty or not. If he protested she said it would do for the times when he had not been found out. At any rate the results equalled those of any high pressure morality seminary in producing men of stability and integrity, and did not interfere with filial affection. There was such impetuosity, generosity, honesty and other qualities, all good, in Grandma that her displeasure was evanescent, her discipline without dregs.

I remember the senna tea. To induce me to drink it a couple of raisins were put in the bottom of the tot. I ran to Grandma on the wings of discovery when I must have been very small to show her I could get the raisins out with my fingers without having to drink the tea.

On the happy day I was confined to the diningroom on the big sofa with some slight indisposition: possibly my nose had again refused to work. There arrived beloved and special guests, among them Dolly Wilson, the friend of my youngest aunt. She produced a child's picture book and spent most of the day on the sofa with me. Here was a new and magical feast in egotism, the undivided attention of a sensitive unselfish adult. She had a gift with children like Uncle Hil's. If we did not waste and batter some of the most precious human qualities, such people would be freed to the task for which Nature anointed them. Most people like children, few are intentionally unkind to them, but the gifted ones have an extra faculty—something different from mere mother love, which can sometimes be so narrow and selfish as to be deleterious. The Dolly Wilsons and Uncle Hils are *en rapport* with the child more entrancingly than child with child: their adulthood gives them the advantage of the angel species.

There was no call for Dolly to waste her visit on a child so luxuriously situated: discipline and relatives would have intervened, but she could spend a day or a year with a child without tedium to herself. I could not be separated from her without an edict from Grandma.

The book was *A Frog He Would a-Wooing Go*, set to music. Page after page he went in big print on musical staves and with bright pictures till a lily-white duck came and gobbled him up—with a roly-poly gammon and spinach, Heigho! says Anthony Rowley. Anthony was an unnecessary intruder who could not be explained, and what was Heigho? A roly-poly was a boiled suet pudding, gammon was ungenteel slang for humbug and heard in the stables or kitchen but not permitted in the diningroom. I was grown-up before I discovered its porcine connection, and had to go abroad to imbibe the culture endemic in spinach.

Oh, that book! I kept it unspotted from the world as an idol till I left it to go abroad. I brought it out to people; but, after Dolly's, their interpretation was feeble and disappointing so it was put away and became dormant.

Ah, Dolly Wilson! How I loved you and love you still in memory with a passionate affection that runs to waste. Do you know of it, there where you have gone? Is there remembrance? Should there be, surely you with Uncle Hil and Aunt Lizzie and her pansies will be waiting among the children's saints.

15

Toys

SANTA CLAUS, the displaced European with his cot-
ton-wool beard and cloak and minus the enchanting
reindeers, is a bore. Toyshops are a phantasmagoria of arti-
ficiality, untidy and inflammable. People have presumed to
pity me that I did not know such joys in infancy. They are
mere make-belief—substitutes. Christmas trees are right for
children in towns confined to snow-buried homes in the
north. The open air furnished with miles of flowers,
streams, orchards and mighty trees was my nursery-play-
ground, and there was a variety of living toys. I deplore the
deprivations of those who have grown up without com-
parable experience. I have been irked by gaps in the education of congenial scholars and philosophers who on step-
ping into the outdoors were unacquainted with a gentian or
a waratah, a woodchuck or an *ornithorhynchus paradoxus*,
a kingfisher or a lyrebird, a vast drove of black swans or
pelicans, the deafening trilling of cicadas or a katydid.
Some of such folk, such affinities in art or philosophy, are
so without gumption that they can be lost between a river
and a telegraph line. To grow up in intimate association

with nature—animal and vegetable—is an irreplaceable form of wealth and culture.

Mother vetoed pets for their own sakes. We were encouraged to care for lost or orphaned and domestic animals and birds, but not allowed to confine or cage them for our pleasure. One day I took from the race that irrigated the vegetable garden a platypus and, clasping it to me, carried it to Mother. It was almost the size of a fat duck without a long neck.

"Dripping all over the floor! What a mess you are in."

My pinafore of snowy linen flounced with *broderie anglaise* and perfectly laundered, really a beautiful sleeveless dress, was drenched. I was eager to lavish on the creature the treatment that more conventional little girls expend on dolls.

"Put the poor little creature back exactly where you found it. It would be uncomfortable here. It doesn't like you to squeeze it like that."

The spiny anteaters, known in the school books as echidnas and colloquially as porcupines, were great favourites. They are endearing in their helplessness and beauty with no protection but to burrow out of sight or to roll in a ball. This saved them from dingoes but not from my fingers, and there is nothing more entertaining than to let one coil on one's fist. Toys were unnecessary with such creatures all about us. The domestic animals were long-suffering with children. Cows were not the only mammals that could be milked. The cats and sluts had no objections to a cuckoo of abnormal size. The mares only were taboo. Their hoofs were dangerous and they were supposed to resent haughtily personal familiarity.

I love pigs. They are companionable creatures and will always respond with almost human grunts to their familiar friends. The tolerant sow stretched out on the straw with her greedy piglets did not resent an addition to the litter.

Little pigs were firm, round and warm in the hands and let forth gorgeous squeals. I would reward the sow by scratching her side with a stick. She expressed her enjoyment by contented grunts. Fleas and an unsavoury odour were a drawback. I would be commanded to take off my boots when approaching the house, and then taken literally by the crop of the neck and plopped in a large pan of water in the back yard and undressed in it to drown the fleas.

"Filthy little puss! I don't know what to make of you! If you can't keep away from the dogs and pigs your father must make you a box in the hen house and you can go and live there."

Enticing prospect. "Can I make a nest like the hens? Can I lay a very big egg?"

The subject had to be turned. I was bidden to care for my neglected doll. I tried to do my duty by dolls and there is an unladylike legend anent. Mother was on guard against irregularities when she saw me inserting dolly under my pinafore; but to inquiry I said, "I'm giving dolly some tummy, like Aunt Ignez does to baby."

Aunt Ignez had low-set breasts.

Wild birds and their nests and eggs were plentiful; even the dream birds, the lyretails, have occasionally been known to feed with the tame hens. I once caught one by hand behind the stables at Ajinby. It had wandered down a slope from its haunts and could not fly uphill to return.

Domestic chicks chipping their shells are an unstaleable delight, and chickens and eggs are a simple right of childhood. The fowlhouses were as commodious as a man's hut. Boxes on shelves around the walls were filled with straw for the layers. There were ladders to reach them. The laity, as distinct from hatchers, had perches in the branches of some not too-high tree. At Ajinby eggs were a staple for Sunday morning breakfast at those times or seasons when a Murray cod had not been procured by night line from the creek or the river. Eggs also appeared at high teas on nights when dinners were not practicable. They were boiled in a saucepan that could hold three or four dozen. Some would be let linger to harden for salads. Or my aunts would carefully crack as many as forty into a buttered dish, season with salt and pepper to bake on coals on the wide white kitchen hearth. Delicious. Often some would have to be thrown out as waste. No one but an infant in the blob stage was restricted to one per meal. Even ladies ate two. Hens would appear with superfluous broods from the wood-piles, or the hay-sheds, from far under the woolshed and many clever hiding places. There were no electric torches to single one out on the roosting tree, so birds for eating often had to be run down. This was diversion for the young, especially the boys. One cousin on a neighbouring station used to shoot some of the wilder birds when they were needed for the pot.

Aunt A., at the head homestead at Bobilla, had an adventurous taste in fowls, not shared by my mother, but much envied by me. In addition to orthodox chooks, she had guinea-fowls and peacocks that screeched, and geese that made the most glorious call, ill-defined as cackling. It always seemed to be the spirit of romance in far places to me and to this day I love it.

Mother objected to guinea-fowls because they were cruel to their colleagues, the ordinary hens. The peacocks were a glory. They scorned the home precincts and took to the bush and flew down as they wished to gobble the grain when it was scarce in winter. They had to be thinned-out by shooting, and their tails companioned the lyrebirds' as decorations. The peacocks' stood higher than even the older children. Every house had several.

We often helped kittens into the world—and saw all

around us mares and cows licking their newly-dropped young. The processes of procreation and birth came to us by natural demonstration without arousing morbid curiosity or obscenity. What need of toys in such circumstances? A rockinghorse would have been superfluous for one whose perambulator was a "waler". Nevertheless, books heighten reality, even for those who live the life depicted. Before I could read, Mother procured for me one of my few juvenile books: *Picture Alphabet of Birds*. Untearable—Mounted on Cloth (T. Nelson and Sons, London and Edinburgh). The price mark 1/6 is still on this priceless treasure. A lonely eagle decorates the front cover, a pelican the back. Both were familiar in my wide natural aviary. Everyone who came had to read the book to me. The albatross represented *A*. His coloured portrait was on one page, a descriptive quatrain on that opposite was exalting to me:

> Spread out thy broad and powerful wings,
>   And hasten o'er the sea;
> What bird, O Albatross, in speed
>   Can hope to equal thee!

The book is still complete, though the victim of rough usage. Those to whom it has been lent, true to their proclivities, have scribbled on it, have torn the pages separate, though no mark was made on it by me.

I was infatuated by animals. I preferred them to children. This was attributed to over-much association with adults. This had other symptoms. One day I took it upon myself to entertain an unprotected guest and reproduced my elders so well that he inquired, "Is she really a child or a dwarf?"

This horrified Grandma. Another manifestation was to the clergyman. Seeking to be congenial by pretended interest in the child, he remarked, "What a wonderful little girl! Will you give me a kiss?"

"No!" was the abrupt reply.

"Why won't you?"

"I don't kiss gentlemen."

"Now who on airth could have told her that?" said the surprised gentleman.

On thinking back it is clear. I was always obedient to physical instruction. My mother was revolted to see old people kissing little children. We kissed chastely if separating for the day or longer and on returning, and, while very small, on going to bed. We did not cling around our parents and hug them. The paternal relatives were even less embracive. My father's eldest brother, a shy kindly gentleman, when leaving home for a week or two would shake hands gravely with all his little ones, even the toddler of two years.

Every now and again it would be considered wholesome for me to be more with people of my own age. Demotion to such company was a sapless exile. Their inanity was inaffable; also I shrank from their roughness. An undiscovered twist to my spine may have increased my abnormal sensitiveness to physical as well as mental pain. I lack the bone and muscle for strength. When I was fully grown any rousing girl of ten could vanquish me in a rough and tumble. Little boys of my own age or slightly older would bang at me with a coat or towel merely in play. The misery of what should have been fun puzzled me as I would steal away alone to endure the agony.

Some children had a habit of pinching, which made me avoid them. I could never pinch hard enough in return with my thin nails to check this degrading practice. A type to be shunned with aversion is the hearty fellow who demonstrates that he is a real man with a noble heart and true by crushing the feeble bones of my hand till I could faint with pain. Some adults of arrested mental development retain the habit of pinching to demonstrate their affection. Thus it was not the minds of adults that alone gave such comfort. They never pinched or hit or insisted on rolling down slopes—another torture. They hoisted me to shoulder or pommel in careful hands that were tender and dependable.

16

Prayer—Efficacy, inefficacy

PRAYERS at Mother's knee were the general intercession, "Gentle Jesus, meek and mild, look upon a little child," the invocation for blessings on parents and others, and the Lord's Prayer. I believed that God was up in Heaven, and heard. An occasion came to give prayer a definite target.

We had been at Ajinby for an extended stay for the birth of a baby. As usual it broke my heart to leave. We set off on a glorious morning on the hard toil over the mountains. The waggonette was attended by the several outriders necessary to apply drags downhill and to steady the vehicle around sidelings. I prayed with passionate intensity for something to ensure return to Ajinby. About noon trouble developed in an axle. A sapling and rope proved ineffectual and, yes, we were actually turning back! My satisfaction amounted to bliss. It was reprieve to me, to Mother merely postponement, involving disorganization of plans and added hard work to her family.

I remember the return at sunset in early summer. The big creek sang my cradle lullaby; the coolness arising from

75

it and the wealth of trees and shrubs after the heat of day,
the roses, the long shades of the hour enfolded me like a
caress. I opened the gate and rushed in. The beloved place
was not as I left it. The front veranda, a spot of special
charm, was invaded by three little boys who sat on the
floor against the wall in abandoned attitudes.

Grandma's youngest sister was not much older than my
mother and had a large brood of ages surrounding mine,
boys in the majority. They were forbidden nothing and
handled knives and tomahawks when other infants were
crawling on the floor. They became the most famous
youngsters of their decade and locality. They were daring
and proficient in forms of mischief normal to the human
male in the grub stage. As they grew, no waterhole was too
deep or dangerous for them to bottom. One of them at the
age of five, proceeding to his first day at school, noted
the tail of a snake protruding from a stone fence, grabbed
it and hung on for a considerable time till someone was
brought to kill it—a large black one.

They were objects of wonderment to me when taken to
visit at their home in town. To reach the nursery on the
upper floor they ascended by the waterpipes and kept up
such a shouting and drumming on the roof and spouting
that Grandma could not hear what her sister was saying.
They were general favourites for their courage, generosity,
gaiety and other qualities, and to the astonishment of the
district reached maturity without being drowned or bitten
by snakes, and in possession of their features and limbs, also
without delinquency.

It was a blow to find such invaders where I reigned un-
challenged amid gentle manners and decorum. They had
too the faculty for catching every distemper such as meas-
les, mumps, chicken pox, etc. To accommodate them their
father had designed a large hospital room in his abode.
Some of the number were at present infected with the dis-

ressing "sandy blight" and to relieve their mother the healthy had been sent to Ajinby as a matter of course to be cared for by my girl aunts, who had just got rid of the turmoil and hard work of my mother's family and a birth.

It was fine weather and the boys led me out of doors to the woolshed and cowyards and other places. The thick white clover was in full bloom. They insisted on rolling in yards of it. I had to do likewise without pleasure and to collect fleas. We had all to be stripped in the back yard and plunged in tubs of water in the laundry before we could appear at the evening meal.

Ten days or a fortnight passed while the axle went to a wheelwright, and we set off again. During this time some of the boys had developed the blight. This prospect had dismayed my mother when obliged to return. We were all clean and healthy when we left Ajinby but during the third day of the journey my sister became afflicted. As usual I escaped all infection. We had spent the previous night at the home of a selector with little children and every one of them contracted the complaint. My mother felt shame and distress all her life to have made such trouble, though innocently on her part. The idea of praying in this connection did not occur to me.

Though I had little time for toys, I had some, and through one that was much prized went to prayer a second time for direct help.

In Grandma's region there had been a church bazaar. A doll was raffled. It fell to Grandma who did not believe in raffles, but had smothered scruples because of the godly purpose. The doll arrived as a marvel from Ajinby on horseback, as carefully carried as an infant by one of the uncles. She was made of sawdust with china head, hands and feet. She had red cheeks and rippling curly hair parted in the middle which I thought was Grandma's because she had irrepressibly wavy hair so dressed. The doll was a bride of the period, the eighties, in pink sateen. She had a train and panniers over a skirt flounced in the front. She was the only doll I ever respected. Her head still reigns as a sitting-room ornament—preserved for me by my mother. I used to sleep with her and she had to be abstracted as her hard head made me uncomfortable and restless. One day I let her drop. One of her hands was broken off above the wrist.

Oh! Oh! To break anything still jars me mentally and physically. This was equal to a major human accident. A little glue would have aided a miracle. A wonder that none thought of it. This was a case for God.

"Mother, can God do everything?"

"Yes, dear, everything. God is all-powerful. That is why you pray to Him, but you must be good, and you must believe."

I believed. I can see my cot now where I placed the doll. I put the severed hand in place and laid the doll at the edge of the bed to assist God. I prayed on my own authority in addition to vespers at my mother's knee, though I do not recollect on what terms, and went to sleep.

I waked early with a sense of something momentous impending. The nursemaid, who shared the room, had already gone out. I turned back the blanket carefully. The doll lay undisturbed, the hand in place but not united.

I no longer believed in the efficacy of prayer, though it remained a habit for many years before it wore away. I have often pondered the promise, "I say unto you, if ye have faith as a grain of mustard seed, ye shall say unto this mountain, Remove hence to yonder place; and it shall remove; and nothing shall be impossible to you."

Who has such faith?

That is the question. Some who come near to achieving miracles by prayer may possess a faint whiff of faith.

17

Ambitions

TWO urgent ambitions concerned animals. My childish fantasies were always of associating with them as equals. I was acquainted with the Biblical legends of the Garden of Eden and of Noah with his Ark. An illustrated family Bible showed Adam and Eve among a variety of animals. All the animals around them and not running away, what an enviable heaven! There were pictures of Una and the Lion, there was glory!

Before I was six I went with my parents to Sydney and was taken to the zoo. At that date I did not warm to the monkeys but I adored the elephant on sight. I had a ride on her. I trotted round to give her an orange, which she took while I got right under her trunk to see what she did with it. I patted her leg and found it warm and soft like parts of other animals. The keeper indulged me because I had no fear and Father gave him half-a-crown. My imagination was stirred beyond containment. I retain my obeisance to elephants, their majestic gentleness, their aristocratic manners.

I became interested in the animals of other lands. My parents found for me a Noah's Ark inhabited by dainty coloured figurines in some kind of glazed pottery. The elephants, giraffes and zebras excited me most. The zebras were beautifully striped but loutishly fashioned by comparison with our own saddle hacks. I thrill yet at the regal grace of giraffes as they are to be seen in some films. Oh, to have known them in their native environment!

I returned to the Biblical illustrations with renewed zest. The familiar domesticated friends, and our quaint native fairies, for a time lost interest. Pictures of St George and the Dragon also engaged my attention and awakened ambition. I conceived a protective interest in the dragon against St George. The dragon was a species of animal and St George merely a man who could do everything for himself. It was the beginning of an unprofitable tendency to sympathize with the underdog—the loser—even the fox.

It was in the days that I used to day-dream of being things at will. No doubt fairytales grew from this state of sprouting imagination. In addition to a desire to live like Adam and Eve among the animals, I longed to fly. I sometimes climbed to roof or post and flapped my arms for practice. I craved also to have a nest like the quail among the stubble, but with eggs big enough for an emu to walk out of full grown.

To be a dragon was the most tempting. I was grounded in the peculiarities of horses. I must keep clear of their heels and refrain from touching their flanks. The dragon, if a snake, may not have excited my partisanship, but he seemed to be a big goanna, and goannas and lizards have always been interesting acquaintances. No revulsion towards them had been implanted in me. I went to Father. It was a winter Sunday morning. The mail had come late on the previous night and he was enjoying a rare moment of ease before the fire with the *Town and Country Journal*.

"Father, why did St George stick the spear down the dragon's throat?" I plopped the book on his knee.

"Um. Ah, let me see. The dragon was covered with horny plates that the spear could not get through. His throat was the only weak spot."

"Then, Father, why was the dragon so silly as to open his mouth?"

"Um, yes, my child! Why? A great deal of trouble would be avoided if we kept our mouths shut."

Pondering the stupidity of the dragon induced a gorgeous fantasy. St George could be vanquished by a change in tactics.

"If I was a dragon St George couldn't kill me," I boasted.

"Couldn't he?" My father chuckled.

"I will be a dragon myself," I announced, growing braver.

Mother, I am sure, never indulged in fantasy. Her natural bent was not that way, and she never had a minute of her own free from supervision or responsibility from the time she could toddle. Life was very wasteful of her outstanding ability and quality. She intervened now. She was taking a peep at *Madame Weigel's Fashion Journal* whence came the patterns used in making her own, mine and the maid's dresses so stylishly and perfectly.

"A dragon is an imaginary reptile. He does not exist. He is something made up in a picture."

"But people in picture-books have turned into cats and ridden on broomsticks."

Probably Mother felt that her censorship had not been sufficiently strict. "Who has been putting silly notions into her head?"

"It's natural to children," said Father. "Till I was quite a man I used to dream of getting in with scientists and inventors to get beyond the earth's attraction to fly to the moon. The marvels in the immensity of space are beyond the human mind . . ."

Mother did not pursue the matter. Father's parents were

Irish. In the estimation of Mother's family that was low socially; intellectually it was half-way to lunacy. My dead grandpapa was of the Herrenvolk. It was necessary to change the subject and let the aberration fade from the child mind.

"I'm going to be a dragon!" I chanted.

"What would you do if you couldn't turn back again?" inquired Mother, in the deflatingly practical way of her side of the house.

"I'd wave a stick and the spell would be taken away, like in the Sleeping Beauty. If I was a dragon . . ."

"You can't be. For one thing, the dragon is *he*, and you are a little *girl*." I had to ponder this. Mother pursued her advantage. "You had better get your slate. You must go to school soon, and you will be all behind like the cow's tail if you can't write."

"I don't do lessons on Sunday."

"Then I'll hear you say your catechism."

Duty called Mother away. "Father, aren't there she-dragons too?"

One day when a male cousin had devastatingly demonstrated what he thought was his sexual superiority in the matter of micturition, Father had satisfactorily and chivalrously explained, "There are little girls and little boys. God made them both, but little girls are much the best."

"Um, what was that?"

"Can't dragons be *shes* as well as *hes*?"

"Yes, to be sure . . . male and female created He them."

This was conclusive. A she-dragon was a full rich daydream, more uplifting than any catechism ever encountered by me, whether secular or sacerdotal. I shouldn't crawl up and open my mouth so that St George could show-off with his spear. I'd turn the other way with my snout under the horse's flank, that sensitive spot that would send him bucking mad any time St George tried to get his spear in my mouth. The horse would be in such a state that Johnny Murphy, my grandma's far-famed horse-breaker, would be thrown. Father, *the best rider in the whole world*, would be the only one who could manage him, and *Father would be on my side!*

Two or three years later when I could read anything and no tome could baulk me, Mother gave me, to indulge my love of animals, Dr Wood's *Natural History*, a nice fat book containing most of the known animals and their pictures. What a treasure, especially as it could be read on Sundays along with delicious little brochures not much larger than a postcard, each about a bird or animal with picture on the cover published at one penny each by the R.T.S. These had been preserved in mint condition from her own girlhood in a way Mother had.

I too cherished my possessions. There was no one to counter what Mother instilled, it became part of my character. It made a problem for me in the matter of books, which I was taught to reverence. It was feared that I was becoming selfish when I hid my books from other children, but it was fastidiousness. I ached to share and to give out other children tore my treasures. It was other children who broke the fragile animals in my Noah's Ark. They tore my book treasures, they slobbered on them, dirtied them, defaced them. They even dismembered them and that stirred me to firm measures. I had no immediate contemporary who was equally interested in Dr Wood's collection. I knew the letterpress about the various animals almost by heart. Had the profession of Quiz Kid been available then I might have won fame in the animal section. The dream of taking up residence with Adam and Eve in their garden had faded. The Zoological Gardens replaced it as a possibility. I read of a multimillionaire who had his own private zoo. That became my newest ambition. I too would become a millionaire and have a zoo of my very own.

18

Education

AS Mother remarked, the time for formal education was drawing near. At the main homestead my second paternal uncle had a famous tutor in charge of his children, Mr Auchinvole. A place had been found for him at Bobilla upon request of one of our leading barrister-politicians, later to become Premier, of whom Mr Auchinvole was a relative or family connection. In his gentleness, his unbreachable good breeding, he was an example of how ineffectual English Public School education could be in fitting a man for life. He belonged to the school who couldn't so much as boil an egg or sew on a button. He would have starved amid tins of food if stranded without a tin-opener, or have gone thirsty beside the purest running water for lack of drinking vessel. In his superior upbringing one thing he had not been taught to do was to abstain from alcohol. So, he was on a remote cattle station hidden in the ranges instead of playing golf with upper middle-class lairds in Scotland.

On Bobilla he was shut away from his enemy unless some new stationhand or mailman, unaware of the crime e was committing, could be engaged to bring a bottle. How it affected the dear man we were too young to know. We were told that Mr A. was indisposed and must not be worried. We had a holiday—where indeed all life, including the schoolroom, was an adventurous holiday.

Though we rode with our elders from early infancy I was not allowed to ride the mile between the two houses. There were cases of children having been dragged in the stirrups. So I had to exercise my legs, my bobbing bonnet watched from home till it disappeared over a rise and in a few minutes I appeared in view of my destination—awaited by Mr A. who described me as "a very small girl, mostly unbonnet, moving at a pace scarcely perceptible."

The house was the good old style that started as a hut, with additions in a string. These were still retained as kitchen, storerooms, meat-room, etc. The house proper had grown later in the same practical way in a long row of additions. The schoolroom was at one end and had a big fireplace for the cold weather. On the veranda outside the door was a small room used as H.M. Post Office. Over this Mr A. presided seriously with government forms, sealing wax, a date stamp and locked waterproof bags.

Aunt and Uncle were a more striking edition of my parents. Father almost reached six feet in his socks, my mother five feet five inches. Uncle was easily six feet, Aunt five feet eight or more. All were slim and straight. Uncle was the most impressive member of his family. He had an eagle profile which went with his haughty bearing and sarcastic tongue. Like all his family he was recklessly hospitable. He sometimes did not know how many guests invited or uninvited would turn up in the diningroom or in the kitchen for meals. He sat at the head of a long table lighted, in days before incandescent lamps, with a stately row of tall brass candlesticks. There he would carve, and carve, and carve for big first and second, and sometimes for three helpings. How he got time to eat anything himself was a miracle. Perhaps that is why he and my father, plus natural slenderness, were always as thin as laths.

Aunt was an exceptional woman. She had a Mac in her maiden name and a charming suggestion of it in her accent which endeared her to Mr Auchinvole. She ran an establishment without conveniences and only "brumby" help that was as full as a beehive and included seven children for whom she made all the clothes for both sexes. My mother would have been a delight as an executant from some *grande couturière*. Aunt could have been a head cutter in some similar establishment. Scissors could not be kept sharp in those far places. Aunt could take a pair of wool shears well-whetted and cut with ease through the tweed to clothe her sons warmly and neatly.

Management at the head station was on a more wholesale scale than at my home. Aunt, in addition to much else, kept abreast of world politics and read Zola, Walt Whitman and others. Her household went on a looser rein than my mother's. These young women pooled their knowledge and resources, isolated as they were from the world. They both had gay flower gardens and must have consulted to enlarge variety, for some flowers appeared in both. Aunt must have taken Mother's idea of correction on the calves of the legs with a sharp switch. But while Mother took evidence exhaustively, Aunt now and again was driven to a clearing up drive. My eldest girl cousin, in recalling those days when she was a merry little sprite, sometimes laughs at the way she would know the signs and escape while the switch promiscuously caught male legs, whose owners, if they were not guilty then, had been much more so than the girls on uncorrected occasions. Rarely, very rarely, as it was a wonder Aunt had a spare moment, we would coax her to play games with us in the dinner hour. Her invention of impositions and forfeits was penetratingly adapted to each

Her clearing-up sometimes had to reach beyond the schoolroom. Odd characters would gather about the hospitable premises. There was a devoted Chinese whose life had been saved by Grandpa; an Indian hawker whose cooking tools had been lost in a flood. For religious reasons he would have been in a pickle, only Aunt lent him some of hers and allowed him to purify them by fire. He had the gratitude of uncommercialized peoples. There was also an old sea captain remittance man who toddled in with a supply of rum and seduced the Chinese and Mr A. It was out of admiration for and cameraderie with the family that the Indian took a small drop, which was his undoing. Uncle was engaged at the other side of the premises. Aunt had her hands doubly full. We children were at large. The mailman waited. I was much titillated to see Mr A., the Chinese, the Indian and Captain—with a bottle protruding from his pocket—sitting on the edge of the veranda, their arms entwined as they swore eternal brotherhood. Aunt swept in and halted appalled at the spectacle and probably at my enjoyment of it.

"Behaving like a grog shanty!" she exclaimed, and sent for Uncle.

He came. No one gainsaid Uncle in his prime, not even a drunk sea captain or a sober upstart. He resembled a Spanish hidalgo in his spurs and leggings, with his efficient horses, his daring dogs. The gentlemen disappeared. Aunt attended to the mail. I was sent home with a note and an escort, to my disappointment.

Bobilla proper and the schoolroom swept Ajinby away from me. My beautiful little sister reigned now as the pet of maternal aunts and uncles. If not out in the world I was at least on the ledge before the nest. I loved lessons in the schoolroom. Four cousins and I occupied it. We sat at a table, one end of which rested against the wall under the window. At the head of it sat Mr A. and in state beside him my cousin A. I sat next to her around the corner with a young cousin and opposite the two elder boys. A. was my senior by enough to give her importance in my eyes. My admiration for her was unbounded. She had grown up with older and younger brothers and was more normally conditioned than I. She had not lived with her grandmother as a pet and a prodigy.

Mr A.'s rule was of the mildest though he kept perfect order. This, on looking back, was due to our home training and his teaching ability, his interest in his charges. The way he brought us on was the envy of other parents similarly situated in regard to the education of their children. He was a gentleman by nature and training, and the gentlest soul alive. He was never known to utter a vulgarism, even when alcohol loosened him to discontent or rebellion against his lot and some of the louts with which it was furnished. One outbreak was so astonishing that it was remembered. A visiting clergyman took it upon himself to admonish Mr A. for his lack of self-control.

"There is lack of self-control in other things," said Mr A. "For example for a man with your income and pretensions to force a family of seven infants on his wife is to me a disgusting lack of self-control."

My parents, and Uncle and Aunt, were exceptional and Mr A. found them so, but what a prisoner-of-Chillon exile it must have been for him!

He had no cane. His mode of punishment was to mete out so many pecks to the culprit. "I'll peck you," he would exclaim.

Pecks were fillips on the cranium. He was a tall man with long fingers with much heavier bones than my father's. The boys used to complain of the unpleasantness of the punishment, but more often of the leniency to girls.

"The girls are pets. It's not fair! They never get pecked no matter what they do."

"The girls do not merit pecks. They are better behaved. They do their lessons properly without mistakes or disobedience."

This made the boys watchful. When we were caught in any irregularity they would promptly point it out. Mr A. would yield to agitation by pecking us too. The boys were still not satisfied.

"Pooh! You only peck them on the pigtail."

Our hair was plaited firmly at the back and fastened with ribbon. It was true that we never were pecked on the head but only on the plaits.

Mr A. gave me a grounding in composition and love of literature, advanced for my age. I gained wider knowledge of the poets. Friday afternoons were a kind of indulgence, perhaps more so to the teacher than to the pupils. The boys did not care for these afternoons. They itched to be abroad on more exhilarating activities. My cousin A. soon escaped them too on the pretext of minding the baby. I was the one who enjoyed the feast. Mr A. indulged the boys with a serial story which was Sinbad the Sailor. They so enjoyed this that they could be bribed to learn a little poetry by heart. I disliked Sinbad. Adventure stories were never my meat. They were so dull. But the Border Ballads and later ones! "On the heights of Killiecrankie, yester morn our army lay"; and "Come hither, Evan Cameron, come, stand beside my knee!"; "Lochiel, Lochiel, beware of the day". There were others, all heady with grief at leaving Scotland for ever. The poor old gentleman would forget he had a listener and nostalgia overcame him. Later I grew to understand the poignancy of "Only in dreams will they see again the outer Hebrides."

Life with my cousins would have been merely an extension of my home life but for my cousin Donald. He was the bane of my life. He was a tease with an uncanny knowledge of his victim's weak spots. He was fiendishly

89

clever too. I was undoubtedly a downy brat for his pluc
ing. My confident boasts of my mother's perfections, a
using at Ajinby, set Don rabidly against me. He proceed
to deflate me. He was ingenious in thinking-up tormen
He had me in agonizing fear of death from lead poisoni
because the house was being painted at the time Mr A
reading lesson was about Painter's Drop, and I had got
speck under my nail. Another day he had a stockwhip a
threatened to shred the kilted skirt of my frock. One of n
hair ribbons came off and he pretended he mistook it f
an old rag and made a whip-lash of it. He took goos
berries into school and put the skins under my chair. I w
dazed when Mr A. remarked on the vulgarity of such
thing on the part of a young lady. I was further perplex
when Uncle from the top of the table one midday sa
what a clever little girl I was to make gooseberry ski
grow on raspberry canes. Again, Don had misrepresent
me. More out of juvenile wit and waggery than a-moralit
he would audaciously attribute all his own misdemeanou
to me. I was so soft and unsophisticated that he really ma
my life miserable. I shrank from going to school. I cried
bitterly that Mother was compelled to consult Aunt.

The switch grew lively in Don's direction. He was n
to be cramped by that. I continued to yowl so constant
that Father at last mentioned it to Uncle. Don was threa
ened with such a father of a skelping as would make
uncomfortable for him to sit down for a time. He w
forbidden to speak to me or to be seen near me, except
school under Mr A.'s protection. It was trying for Au
with all she had to contend with, to have such an infant
addition, though no hint of this was ever conveyed to n
by her nor any of my cousins. Aunt and I were frien
from the beginning because she had a dignified grown-
way of talking to me, which won me.

Don was too resourceful to be squelched or robbed

his sport. He could convey to me without being heard or seen that I was a sneaking tell-tale, a little crybaby, and all sorts of things opprobrious at our time of life. Uncle came on the scene again and gave the imbroglio close attention. His report was that he was willing to skelp Don into subjection but that it was useless. We could not be separated. Don under penalty of corporal punishment could be forced to ignore me but I was a free agent and at every opportunity would seek him out. Uncle, of course, could not skelp me. He threw the problem to my mother. She talked seriously to me.

"You see, you *are* silly. You don't keep away from Don. Auntie has too much to do. If you keep on acting like a baby you won't be able to go to school to be taught by Mr Auchinvole. You must not be a trouble to Auntie. She is very good to have you there."

This was the first hint I ever had that I might be a trouble to anyone, or be excluded from their company as unwelcome. It was sobering. Mother continued,

"All boys are teases. You'll have to endure them or keep away from them. You love your uncles at Ajinby, but when I was a girl they used to torment me much more than Don does you. You can't be a baby any more. You are a big girl."

This sank in, especially as Mother concluded, "A. never cries about Don. Why can't you be like her? She takes no notice of him."

Too young to adduce that Don took no notice of A., this braced me because A. had become to me a model and an ideal in her advanced accomplishments.

The memory of how the trouble resolved itself is lost. The boys were absorbed in station doings, I became an outgrown interest. Don was the only trial I encountered in my first decade and it was of short duration and quickly dispersed. On looking back I see that he badgered me but

91

he never pinched me or was physically cruel to me or I should have avoided him with fear and abhorrence.

We left Bobilla not long afterwards. I did not return on a visit till I was grown-up. The last part of the journey was on horseback. The baby of the family had sent her saddle hack, Prince Charlie, an old blood of exquisite paces, and my cousin A. had contributed her beautiful saddle. A tinge of the old attitude disturbed me when I saw it was Don who had come with one of his sisters to meet me. I had a sizeable Gladstone and there was no pack-horse in sight. I quailed, thinking that Don would regard me as a pest that had merely enlarged since childhood. This was dispel'ed when it came to light that he would delegate the task to no one else. He was demure during the call on my mid-way hosts but as soon as the big white entrance gates closed behind us the old blague broke out, though the plant had matured, the fruit was riper today. A few years had made a change in me too. Today we could play in the same game—not equally matched as I was never on a level with my cousins or of members of my own family; but at least I was a player and in no danger of being pierced.

Don was now a caballero. His spurs and leggings gleamed, his gear matched his horse, and that was safe only for experts to mount. I was apologetic for my luggage but Don mounted with it as easily as if it had been a lady's handbag. The horse protested, Don waved the portmanteau around his head and then it rode in front of him without even a restraining strap up and down the passes as safely as I had done as a baby on the pommel.

The small boy's diablerie had ripened to humorous wit. Don's inventiveness in "chaff" was now without sting. The boyish pranks had been symptoms of an embryo ladies' man. He was prolific in hoaxes. Always a good mark, I would be led into half-a-dozen a day and they were so unny that I enjoyed them as much as anyone. Don the ormentor was equally diligent today as a gay and inventive 10st. We reminisced with the zest of old-timers. Don had a knack in seizing the ridiculous aspect of an incident, and at he date was manipulating a farce. There was about the tation a shy and sawny youth who confessed to Don his ears and hopes regarding girls. They were rare treasures nd always snapped from him by men more skilled and ttractive; as, for instance, Don himself.

"What you need to rectify your state is a matrimonial gency," advised Don, and was forthwith entrusted with he affair. Don was indulging his propensities alone till one f his sisters suspected what was going on and admitted is to the entertainment. Love affairs were not treated eriously, but merely as incidents. If unsuccessful they ad to be surmounted without hysteria or any tragic lummery.

Don's performance was exploded by Aunt. Still in her rime with grown daughters to take much of the care of he house from her, she had more time for reading and vorld politics. But she remained at the head of her domin-on and every now and then would clear up the North-west rontier as we termed it in days when that imperial trouble pot was familiar in the news. During an inspection she was urprised to find a photograph of the beautiful girl who ad been her bridesmaid on the bedroom table of a casual and about the place.

"How did that get out of my album? Who would dare to heddle with it?"

It was discovered to be "one of Don's pranks". The hoto was restored to its proper place, Don adjured to keep is clowning within reason. Aunt handled the situation with he tolerance and shrewd understanding of the days of the witch or the dispersal of the miscellany of gentlemen who ad disfigured her front veranda. Her sense of humour and interest in life remained with her till she was over ninety, still erect and stately, and the prized companion of another generation of mischievous wits and wags in the making. She had prestige as one of the genuine pioneer ladies of the squatting days who had early brought culture to the primordial fastnesses.

19

Change of residence

WE left Bobilla.

The maid and I rode on horseback, I on a lady's
ack given to me by my grown-up cousin Joe and named
ephyr to describe her paces. The maid had Jenny Lind, a
ll brown mare as swift as the wind, on whom I had many
gallop. We met two trappers as we descended from our
ountain fastnesses. They had long sticks like the carrying
mboos of the Chinese, on which were slung scores of
retails on the way to market. They had already shipped
any hundreds overseas. They were Americans. They were
lmired as enterprising. I don't recall any protest or ex-
ressions of regret for the vandalism. The gullies were still
ive with these fey creatures. They played across the road
d disappeared among the underbrush in the old familiar
ay as we travelled.

Our new home was in the flatter, more lightly-timbered
ountry. Its situation near to schools and railways and
wn had advantages, but I never forgave it for its inferior-
y to my birthplace. Its first sight filled me with a sense of
esolation. The trees were not so majestic. The ranges

were low and ragged without gorges and mighty rock
like castles and cascading streams draped with tree-fern
and maidenhair and flowering shrubberies along their banks
No lyrebirds gambolled across the track to flute in euca
lyptus aisles across a big singing creek. Oh, Ajinby, with
its river, its creeks, large and small, full of fish, its wealth
of orchards and ornamental trees, its flower gardens with
pomegranates and magnolias! Here there were no rocks o
ferns at all. There were no permanently running creeks
only weedy waterholes. Mother named the place Stillwater

Also, a cavalryman was being demoted to association
with the infantry. Only men rode in the new district, and
they merely poked about on mokes. I was so much in
harmony with the gaits of horses that bolting, shying, rear
ing or other mild antics had never unseated me. The nearest
I came to a tumble was when riding in one of our new
paddocks. The light soil was prone to erosion. Rains ha
washed a pothole leaving the crust of the track unbroken
The horse, strange to that soil, cantered onto it. It gav
way beneath his hooves, all four, and deposited him in th
hole as neatly as if packed there. I was set upon the earth
unjarred, unhurt, with the reins in my fingers. To regai
my seat I should have had to sit down as on a hassock. Th
gentle well-mannered beast was so surprised that it wa
laughable. He stood as if paralysed, trembling in every fibr
as only a horse can tremble if fear does not drive him t
panic flight. He had to be petted and assured that all wa
well, whereupon he regained poise, climbed out of the hol
and went on our way with the shir-r-r to be interpreted a
well-being.

Funnier was the mishap to my uncle's grand Bobill
horses when he visited us at the same time. Released afte
hard travel they hurried to drink at the deep weedy water
holes, and strode in. They disappeared, down, down in un
dignified dives—to come up snorting and terrified.

The new land, so drab and unspectacular at first sight,
dually disclosed more favourable features. Koalas were
great numbers. They wailed in the trees at night like in-
ts being tortured. When they were passing from one tree
another we could often catch them, for they are among
 mildest of wild things. In fact they are as intimate as
-dogs. Contemplate a heavy animal with claws so power-
that he can climb a hard slippery eucalyptus trunk and
sp the branches so firmly that a gale will not dislodge
, yet he can be picked up without fear of injury and
dled by a child. The spiny anteaters were so plentiful
t we set them in lines to run races at their own pace,
ich is that of the tortoise.

he native cats were a definite excitement. We had not
n familiar with them at Bobilla because of the variety
dogs that abounded. At Stillwater they would clear a
st in a night, leaving piles of corpses with only the
od sucked from their necks. They were long-snouted
 bloodthirsty with dark soft coats dotted with white
 hailstones. Firm defensive measures were necessary.
e free birds, including the turkeys, had to be confined to
cific roosting trees, the trunks of which had wide col-
 of tin. Ladders that helped the birds up were taken
 y after dark. The fowlhouse also had to be covered with

he men laid traps to lessen the pests. We would find as
 y as six or eight dead at a time. With the lack of
eamishness of our years, we used to rifle the pouches of
 females for the rows of kittens like hairless mice. What
 rious furs these cats would have provided. Mother made
ittle tippets and muffs for frosty days, but no one then
 there wore fur coats. There were several other species
marsupials in plenty with larger and more durable pelts
 the cosy rugs for buggy or bed or opulent floor mats.
ere were also many kangaroo rats like miniature kanga-

roos which made cosy nests in tussocks. We'd chase
rats out on frosty mornings and put our hands in
warmth they had left. In the waterholes were a few ⟨
that had silky dark-brown pelts like mink. All these sm
creatures were the perquisites of the older boys who ki⟨
them in imitation of their fathers with the larger anim
The adult tanners used wattle bark. Skins so cured w
soft and among the best specimens of the tanning art to
found. The effect was lasting and did not perish or stif⟨
the pelt.

We children tanned our skins, bird or animal, with a⟨
and had some fine results, also some strong smells wo
emanate from storeroom or laundry where we would ⟨
them green with the salt and alum inside. We had to
watchful or we would lose them in the interests of hygie
Those wasted skins would bring large sums today wl
much poorer furs are beyond the means of all but th
with high wages.

I never saw a native cat after that. Since their extermi⟨
tion the imported foxes have increased to take their pla
and to make secure fowlhouses still a necessity.

One day in later years in Chicago I met one of
McCormick ladies wearing a beautiful fur coat that so t⟨
my taste that I stroked it, remarking "It's exactly like
native cats of my childhood."

"I'm interested to hear that. I have never seen anot⟨
coat like it. The fur people can't place it, but wher
bought it in Vienna they told me it was Australian v⟨
cat."

How came pelts of a kind rarely skinned by us for ⟨
purpose purchasable in Europe by a millionairess nea
twenty years later?

20

Return to paradise

A WONDERFUL thing happened soon after removal to our new home. Grandma arrived. Three of us were now of an age to undergo formal schooling and she had brought my sister home for that purpose. There was a second reason for her visit connected with an impressive old lady, new to us, who followed the vocation of midwife. An addition to our family was imminent, and, due to the removal and other worries of which I knew nothing, Mother was feeling the strain more than usual.

Three years of separation and applied education among older children, while my sister had occupied my place at Bjinby, had not cooled my attachment to Grandma or to Bjinby. My one obsessing thought and determination was to accompany her on her return. No Peri could have pleaded more passionately at the gates of Paradise. The plea was heard. Why, is not clear. One of the advantages in removal was the regular school which yawned for us and for whose discipline I was ripe. From something overheard on a visit to a neighbour, who had also migrated from the superior area of Monaro, it appears that I may have been

99

considered so "bright" that I could overtake the othe
pupils. Mr Auchinvole would have fostered this notion. H
contempt for the plebeian form of education awaiting m
after his private personal teaching amounted to irration
jealousy.

After some weeks that dragged on my patience we se
off. Delight, anticipation of adventure, contentment re
awakened in me the moment we were in the buggy t
begin the journey. Never again was I to know such nou
ishing, releasing satisfaction on so many emotional prong
Grandma had not denied me. I was with her. I was goin
back to Ajinby with her. *Back to Ajinby with Grandma*!

On a piercing winter day we crossed the plains to th
tiny railway station where we waited at a wayside pub fe
the Southern Mail to pick us up in the small hours of th
dark. The working man drove us. Father was up the cour
try on business concerned with his new venture in life.
remember the exciting nearness to the panting engines th
halted in the station during the night. Their grinding an
huffing, the clank of the couplings of the trucks, were a
obbligato to my inner fire. And then we were sitting i
our carriage wrapped in possum rugs with a foot-warme
our luggage piled about us and a picnic feast provided b
Mother in a box.

Away we rumbled with splendid whistles and snorting
through the darkness on the wings of expectation. W
changed trains at Cootamundra and saw Father for te
minutes. On again till there came a jolting and rockin
then a crash and a rough full stop. Men ran about an
shouted to each other. There was movement and openin
of doors and windows on each side of us. Grandma ha
grown hard of hearing and anxiously questioned those wl
knew no more than she.

"Find out if there is any danger," she bade me.

A stentorian voice with the individualistic squatter authority in it roared from the adjoining carriage, "Danger, Madam, the only danger is that we'll be stuck here without anything to eat!"

It was a crisp frosty morning. The breath of the lady in our carriage issued visibly from her nostrils. She was *breathing*! No danger of her dying.

Soon we could climb down to discover what had happened. A level stretch of road bed had saved us from possible disaster. The engine had left the line for many yards to bump into a coal-shed at a little siding on the road to Gundagai. All the carriages were upright, the end one only half-off the rails. The engine seemed to hate the coal-shed. It was banged hard against it shrieking in rage, spouting fire and boiling water from which we were warned. At home we had left bleak winter paddocks. Here the white clover was already ankle-deep, first symptom of the lusher region to which we were bound. I had no interest in the cause of the engine's aberration. The incident enhanced the bliss in which I stewed.

My second uncle met us at Gundagai to save Grandma the coach journey. We rattled behind a spirited pair which filled me with satisfaction as another sign of the more opulent way of life of Ajinby. In the new district people drove only one horse in a buggy—quite declassé. We spent the night in Grandma's town cottage. Grandma and Uncle talked above my head. There was business to conduct on the following morning, so we reached Ajinby after dark. The household and watchdogs came out to meet us. I rushed inside. There was the familiar dining table, gleaming and laden. A great fire of logs was crimsoning in the hearth. Grandma's basket chair stood in the corner near it with a candle on an attachment on either side. There she would read the newspapers in a searching and able manner for information on markets, prices and anything in connection with the management of her property. She read the local journal for association and news of those whom she knew. I never saw her read anything but documents, newspapers, the Bible and the prayerbook. So little do youngsters know of their elders that I put her down as a non-reader. It was only in recent years that my uncle related that she had been an omnivorous reader in her young days, but once she found herself reading to the postponement of some duty and was so shocked that from that day she abjured reading or what was "not true" as a semi-sin, and a dangerous self-indulgence. Thereafter she read only as I had noted.

In the morning I was out betimes to inspect my kingdom. In three years it seemed to have shrunk slightly. Orchards and buildings were not big enough. But the deciduous trees which embowered it were still leafless. When last seen they had been in full leaf and flower, or heavily fruited. I ran everywhere to each beloved nook: to the stables and harness and salt rooms, to the hay-shed and cowyards and woolshed, to the laundry and dairy and fowlhouse, the blacksmith shop, the vehicle sheds, and all sorts of nooks. The earth was seething with spring. As the leaves opened, the hops on Mother's beloved elm-trees, the catkins on the long mermaid skipping-rope tresses of the weeping willow, made the old place itself again.

Up in the cow-paddock beyond the hay-shed was an indigenous flower garden, acres square. Early came the harbingers and flycatchers, cowslips and big yellow soldier's buttons. The tiny hard kind (*leptorrhynchus squamatis*) with its wiry stem and the hard button on the end was excellent for threading the tiny pink or white convolvulus to make a lady dressed in flounces. The woolly everlasting (*helichrysum semipapposum*) and the bigger *podolepis acuminata* and others of the daisy tribe were in many varieties. The ordinary purple violet was companioned by the purple fringed (*thysanotus tuberosus*) like a fairy's iris. The fairies' orchids were in great variety and beauty, delicate and unique. Little birds hung their nests in the remaining clumps of thorny bushes (*acacia juniperina*). Uphill outside the cowpaddock was wild and splendid with the big everlastings and *exocarpus cupressiformis* with its funny little cork-like cherries, and a lone kurrajong or two. Far down by the creek was a paradise of purple aromatic *prostanthera* and the white teatree and here and there the tall white banksias and a variety of grevilleas and perfumed clematis. The thrushes sang madly as they nested in the fragrant sweet briars along the roadside. Heaven could be no more magical and mystical than unspoiled Australia. Chicks, foals, calves, lambs and other young things were part of the scenery. All the old delights remained. Others became apparent with my ripening understanding and affections.

Since my last visit my eldest uncle and the aunt next to him had both been married. Uncle lived four or five miles distant, Aunt about ten miles away. This meant a charming new auntie and uncle and two more homes to visit and enjoy. There were still two aunts and two uncles with Grandma.

I was considered backward with the needle for my age so Grandma set me to darn my stockings. This was an easy exercise and my proficiency a year later won the prize for darning against adults at the district Agricultural Show near my new home, which went to my head.

I contracted ringworms. As an unclean creature I was handed over to Grandma. My competent aunts and the maid and other help had long since relieved her of any supervision of the house. Her unsleeping energy was available for prodigies of repairs and emergencies. The ringworms put me in all three classifications. To save the innocent from contamination I had to bathe morning and afternoon in a tub set in one of the storerooms among the light

103

harness and ladies' saddles. Being a pariah was most enjoyable. It brought exclusive attention from Grandma which was rather a rise than otherwise socially, and I was a sop to Grandma's habit of industry.

"Dirty child! I wish I could make you more genteel. You must have been kissing the calves again. You are much too grown-up now for such antics."

I had outgrown the society of the pigs, but it was true that I still enjoyed the contact of the warm fragrant hide or fleeces of my daily companions.

The ringworms were confined to my scalp. There were three in the thick fine hair that was kept clipped at the level of my shoulder blades. One of the Uncles suggested that my poll should be shaved.

"Better not risk it," said an aunt. "It would be terrible if her hair would not grow again. We could not face her mother."

The family had had enough of my baldness.

Grandma made an ointment of coal tar, sulphur and mutton fat. She dumped me on a block in the middle of the back yard encased in a sheet, and clipped the hair closely from the three virulent spots, each nearly as large as a shilling. The ointment was applied in neat little pads covered as trimly as a trivet with thick calico and the hair plaited tightly over. This treatment twice a day was effective. The evil did not spread, no scar remained, no white hairs appeared. That was the only ill-health my scalp has known to date. A tradition that my locks should never be trimmed except to level the ends hardened in the family. No matter how I pleaded to have short hair like other girls, to be relieved of the burden of increasing clouds of hair, my mother would never consent, and I lacked the daring to take the scissors without permission.

21

Religion and democracy

THE Rector came once a month from Gool Gool to stay the night and conduct service in the drawing-room on Sunday morning. On other Sundays Grandma deputized for him, not a sermon, a psalm, a lesson, or a collect missing. "What ever your hand finds to do, do it with all your might."

My aunts in turn acted organist at the piano with something from *Hymns Ancient and Modern*. When tiny I used to reap rewards for sitting still and abstaining from acting curate to Grandma. Foremost was a pomegranate which I could nurse, and, after church, eat the little bit of jelly in which the seeds were embedded.

"I cannot understand your appetite for the silly things—nothing but seeds," my friends remark today.

But, ah! to me there is incomparable beauty in the contours and tints of their tough hides and in the colour of the jelly. They have the magic of Aladdin's lamp to transport me the long, long journey back to that dainty old room, warmed by natural family affection that never wavered, never waned, as well as a fire of red-gum logs. The

105

hearth was guarded by a fender and fire-irons with brass ornamentation and a magnificent white angora hearth rug which I though the height of grandeur. I was allowed to sit on a hassock with my feet in the fur. The pomegranates were preserved as a decoration on a corner table with other objects alluring to me. One of the doors opened on to the veranda and the flower garden. On summer mornings I could watch the butterflies on the old-fashioned flowers such as honesty and love-lies-bleeding. I particularly cherished two specialities. A plant of box, such as is to be found edging garden beds, had grown taller than I and was trimmed in a round head. Long after I was to see similar box-trees grown high as elms in the town of Hitchin, Herts. But I imagined Grandma's specimen to be a little girl tree among the regal giants to be seen farther away across the creek, where the lyrebirds fluted. Beside it was the Parramatta rose, so-called because Great-grandma had brought one of its like from that direction in early days. The buds were encased in a firm netting like the lattice on some wine bottles. I do not recall that it had a perfume or that the buds were prickly like moss roses. I have never seen another of its kind elsewhere. Perhaps it blooms in the gardens of Uncle Hil and Aunt Lizzie in the Unknown Places.

A further concession to infant frailty was a brooch that Grandma wore constantly. A blue stone was set in a fretwork of gold—an ornamental and useful piece of jewellery. It must have been an amethyst but in certain lights it was indistinguishable from a sapphire, and all sorts of objects were enhanced through its facets while the sermon droned on and on unabridgedly. These treasures, as well as the Chinese nest of eggs brought back from some exhibition, remained; but I was no longer a toddler, nor even a child. I was a *big girl*. I had now to do my own hair. Governessing me was an imposition on my aunts' leisure. I must stick to my lessons and practise the piano assiduously. Only on that understanding had I been allowed this sojourn. Grandma took charge of the physical and moral part of my training. She put me rigorously through the catechism on Sunday mornings after breakfast, with trimmings, a full hour which prepared me for the church service.

There is in circulation much sentimental twaddle, dubious and debilitating, about the repressions suffered by children of my mother's generation from parents and others. Mother's immediate family during my first ten years contained eight uncles and aunts. Grandpapa and a beautiful aunt of twenty-two years died before I knew them. Great-grandmama was still alive when I was tiny and Great-grandpapa, though dead, still reigned in reference and reminiscence in the consciousness of his descendants as a "real old John Bull". In addition to Grandma I had the equivalent of seventeen other grandparents in her eight sisters and brothers and their spouses, all of whom I knew and remember. With some of them I was warmly intimate. For these I had deep affection, slighter for those not so closely acquainted. There was only one who was beyond the pale. He was a mistake—the tragedy of the great-aunt who married him late in life. This group, in some ways not wholly congenial to my young uncles and aunts, was flippantly referred to as "The Tribe", though not in Grandma's hearing.

On my father's side were two grandparents and ten uncles and aunts. All these relatives had the same tribal status. Not till we young fry were grown-up did we know the difference between blood aunts and uncles and their in-law spouses. There were also squads of Mother's cousins and some of Father's nephews and nieces in the age bracket of uncles and aunts and just as affectionately regarded, and all of whom lived up to their status in affection and kindly interest. Half of these people at least, on the maternal side, were dogmatic. They were often stubbornly and ignorantly opinionated, brusque, limited, uncompromising, but free from malignancy. There was deafness in the family and no neighbours to be considered. They were barnacled individualists and expressed themselves without physical or mental soft-pedals, but no youngster ever came to grief through expressing his opinion too. Each and all were allowed to make explanations or to formulate ideas. Suppressed! Quite the reverse. Uncle John (we did not say great-uncle or great-aunt, they were uncles and aunts *per se*), was asked by the proprietors to give a testimonial for some nostrum—"I have tried your remedy and found it as effective as a plaster on a wooden leg."

The qualities most commended were honesty and truth. Quibblers who would hum and haw or sly fellows who spoke with split tongues were abominated. Jealousy, sulks or a lack of cheerfulness were not tolerated in my immediate family. Mother regarded jealousy as dementia. She watched for it in us and was very wise in giving no cause for it. I never knew which were her favourites among us— if any. She never made a slip in the matter. My father would have been incapable of the cruelty of exalting one child above another. This of course did not extend to the babies who were idolized by all of the elder ones. This obtained with my grandma and uncles and aunts too. They held the balance without a mistake between us all. To grow up in such an atmosphere was surely good fortune, though it left us lacking in protective chicanery and cunning to succeed in the world or to make business pay.

I leant against Mother's knee to imbibe Dr Watt:

> We only need labour as hard as we can
> For all that our bodies may need. . . .

I always rushed ahead to insert after the first line, "For we cannot work harder than that."

Mother said as I knew that hymn I could learn another;

108

" 'Tis the voice of the sluggard, I heard him complain," had more substance. The "Old Hundredth" seemed to be faulty logic, praising God, "Without our aid he did us make". How could we help God to make us before we existed? The clergyman at that date was a little Irishman so understanding as to laugh with me at the joke. He said we'd omit that verse.

Before I was ten I became critical of the anthropomorphic God as interpreted in the churches. I did not warm to One thus revealed as the semblance of a bullying and mean old man who must have all his own way, be praised all the time and for attributes which were deplorable in us.

As soon as I could read I took the chapter of the Bible, set for Sunday study, verse about with Mother. This ran by with more satisfaction in the exercise of reading than of interest in the subject matter. I was enjoined to read in addition a chapter by myself morning and evening, one from the Old Testament, the other from the New. The horror of Christ's agony on the Cross took hold of my imagination not only as wicked and cruel beyond computation but also foolish when God, the all-powerful, could have changed everything by raising his hand. Why did he allow his dear son to suffer so horribly to save us? Stupid! This was proved in mankind, still being so evil that they had to be groaned over continually and put in jail and hanged. Surely God who knew everything and could do everything would have known that. The doctrine of free will was beyond my infantile grasp. This was a big trouble. I took it to Mother. She was most sympathetic. She said when she had been a little girl she had suffered similar distress and used to weep her heart out for the agony of the dear Saviour.

"We must not expect to know all the mysteries of life at once. Many of them will have to wait till we get to Heaven.

Everything will become clear to our understanding in the hereafter."

That was alleviating. Not only children but adults find relief in the mere telling of their distress to a sympathetic listener. Someone to tell it to is one of the fundamental needs of human beings.

A lesser matter puzzled me. There was a prayer for the Royal Family in the church service in which the princesses were listed. It occurred to me that princesses must be a species of girls. I ran to Mother.

"Mother, are princesses girls?"

"Yes. What else could they be?"

"Really, truly girls?"

"Of course."

"Like me?"

"A bit better than you, I hope."

"Are they little girls?"

"At first they are—like every other little girl."

"Do they do everything the same as other little girls?"

"Yes."

"Do they eat and have a bath and go to bed?"

"Yes."

"And say their prayers?"

"Yes indeed, little princesses always say their prayers."

"Do they eat breakfast and dinner?"

"They could not live without eating."

Princesses were clearly girls. I gathered my wits to have one more point settled. Queen Victoria was a revered entity, something like Grandma, only on a throne. Reticence were part of refined living. In their inculcation delicacy was sometimes burdened with shame. Such a basic and vulgar thought could only be whispered, even to my mother I approached.

"Mother, can I ask you anything I like?"

"Yes, my dear. I hope you will always come to me first

110

and ask me anything you want to know, and I'll tell you if I can."

I sidled near, hand over mouth, eyes downcast, abashed, but spurred by curiosity.

"What is it? Take your hand away from your mouth, and don't whisper and mutter like rude boys."

In those days to whisper behind the hand was socially as unacceptable as "to shoot the words out of the side of the mouth" is today.

"Look at me. What do you want to know?"

"Mother, if princesses are really little girls do they have to go to the lavatory or take senna tea like I do?"

"Yes, my dear. Of course they do. God made all little girls, and he made them all alike. The only difference between princesses and other little girls is that they live in England, in a grand house called a palace, and you live in a little house in Australia with me."

I skipped away. Any pomp of circumstances in an emperor or a lord mayor, any pretentious assumptions of physical superiority on behalf of the most bedizened great ladies dispersed into thin air for ever.

The grief over Christ was ameliorated, but everything that pastors and masters promulgated increased God's unpopularity with me as judged by human standards. So on a Sunday morning at Ajinby, vividly remembered, I came to issues with Grandma. The weather was grey and wintry. Everything had been burnished for God's day. I can still see the inner back yard, clean swept. Not a footmark or leaf lay upon its smooth face, nothing but one puddle in a depression after the night's rain. I was enjoying a respite after catechism. Church was imminent. Grannie, who was sitting in the roofed pergola (it was called the awning) outside the kitchen, was putting a mark in the book she had been reading—probably the impending sermon. Louie, the maid, was taking off her apron, disclosing her Sunday dress.

111

I was nursing a doll. These effigies had little charm for me but dolly seemed preferable to sitting bolt upright and still for an hour, a big girl now, not to be placated by pomegranates, or even the Chinese eggs.

"I'm not going to church today, Grandma."

"What's this I hear! You must worship your God."

"How do you know God is here?"

"God is everywhere. . . ."

"But Grandma, how do you know? No one has ever seen him."

"What has got into your froward heart? ! ! !"

"I don't believe he is here. I am tired of him."

"You must love and worship your God all the days of your life.".

"But I *don't* love him!"

This was too grave for argument. Grandma took the big millet broom from beside the kitchen door and laid me flat on the earth, almost in the puddle. I was wearing a dress that lay perfectly in the pleats of the kilted skirt, a fine example of Mother's skill with her wonderful American sewing-machine that had been carried over the ranges on a pack-horse, not so trustworthy as the dray had been for the piano. The treadle had been broken and the work of the blacksmith who mended it "as good as new" is still to be seen.

The dress on which I must put no spot and which only for Sunday wear could be exposed without a pinafore, had an inch or two of mud on the hem. I confronted Grandma, astonished and indignant.

"Look what you've done to my best dress! I'll tell Mother!"

Grandma's reaction to the counter charge I do not recall. Her landing on me with the broom contained no sting. She was always impetuous and never mean. No misdemeanour was held against me for more than a day.

I remember finding myself locked in the pantry, the one outside the diningroom which had held the grog for the barman in shanty days. There I was to stay without anything to eat till my *froward* heart returned to God. I loved this pantry. It had shelves right up to the ceiling along the end and in the embrasures of the diningroom chimney. The shelves were packed with interesting articles. In here were kept certain stores such as the tin of sweets, essences and spices, and special preserves. There was little floor space left. Under the window was a table on which my aunts put last touches to cold puddings or cakes or bouquets, sometimes touches they wished to be a surprise. Therefore I was often shut out, and in any case there was not enough room for an extra. Now I had the tempting cubby all to myself. The vases were an attraction, a variety of many colours, shapes and sizes, from glass slippers to an epergne. In some of these my aunts arranged flowers freshly cut each day. To retain them longer than a day would have been considered as frowsy as uncombed tresses. They made the house a perfumed bower and when tossed over the garden fence wilted to fertilize the gooseberries' domain. My elder aunt arranged violets in the glass slippers. They were adult size and it took an hour to pluck enough from the mats of violets that grew under the lilacbush and elsewhere. To handle these at my leisure was reward enough for the incarceration.

Whether I returned to God, or my aunts feared for their vases, or Grandma forgave me unconditionally because she grew weary of the discipline before I did, has dropped from memory. I can't recall ever having gone without a meal unless too absorbed in other matters, or for self-discipline, or to do something more exhilarating with the money saved; but never from poverty or for punishment. No doubt Sunday dinner from rich natural materials undeteriorated by preservatives or standardized processing helped me to see the error of my budding thought. Those dinners! Healthy, well-exercised poultry or other meats, selected fruits and vegetables fresh from virgin soil, cream from unforced cows, my aunts' pastry made with butter and so light that the men claimed it should be eaten in a nosebag to prevent it from floating away. The technicality of no Sunday cooking was evaded by the aid of the brick oven, the maw of which demanded as many as four dozen eggs for the biscuits alone that replenished the tins after each Saturday's baking. This cavern was like a thermos, so that a touch on the fire in winter brought dishes baked overnight to the table piping hot.

Such a grounding in choice provender ill-prepared me for the inferior rationing ordinarily encountered in the world. No highly condimented sauce will disguise for me that a sausage made from giblets, or scraps of codfish soaked in all the wines of France, are anything but offal no matter how haughtily claimed as recherché or sophisticated European cooking. My powerful and sensitive sense of taste cannot become reconciled to the flavour of poultry hung or frozen undrawn, nor meats slightly decayed. It took years of deprivation to inure me to fruits ripened off the stem. Freezing of various kinds also deteriorates food for those who have been used to better.

My dissatisfaction with God was shelved for the moment, but it was the early symptom of a questioning mind, that heaviest of handicaps in the struggle for worldly success or mental complacency. Such a mind is driven by inner standards that cannot accept the assumed powers of any vicariously to grant indulgences or promise forgiveness for lapses of integrity: a mind dependent on its own search for God and open to the discovery that it takes a greater mind to find God than it does to lose him, a mind with austere, demanding, lonely standards that call for fortitude, and fortitude is a great absentee.

22

Snakes

MY freedom from certain fears does not include tolerance of snakes. From infancy my elders implanted in me their own fear of these reptiles and it took root and grew to an unconquerable revulsion. Even pictured snakes horrify me; the presence of one where I could not escape would surely reduce me to a paralysed jelly in terror. Today in areas where snakes are not known the slightest rustle in grass or underbrush will cause me involuntarily to spring away from it.

"Dear me, what a state your nerves must be in!" someone will remark, but it is merely that revulsion has become a reflex action.

Ours was not a snake-infested region, though in summer a week would seldom pass without seeing one or sometimes several. Those acquainted with Lakes Cargelligo and Illilliwah and such inland areas would reminisce of innumerable snakes. Thousands would be slaughtered without perceptible decrease, so that one wondered what they lived on, for they are not discredited as cannibals. It must have been hard on the frogs. I am thankful that I have not had to reside in those parts of the continent where pythons or carpet-snakes are valued as mice-killers and kept in store-rooms as pets. A Queensland girl friend told me she was so fond of her carpet-snake that when she found it coiled on a flourbag in its residential quarters she would stroke it in passing as one does a cat. Our north is afflicted with the taipan, whose deadliness is increased by his aggressiveness, and fills me with terror of going to those fair regions.

Ours were of the shy variety, clever as conjurors in disappearing. They never attacked unless molested or cornered. I know of few horses or dogs that died by their fangs and fewer human beings who have been bitten. When picnicking we'd sometimes find their last year's sheath, a complete replica, even to scales and eyes in what looked like cellophane. So unrelaxing was the war against snakes that the settlers would nearly tear their houses down to dislodge one from the foundations or the eaves where they liked to take refuge. It was disconcerting to see a snake's head come through a crack in the veranda or protrude beside your legs if sitting on its edge. A settler near us one day saw a deadly tiger-snake extrude its head onto the doorstep, whereupon she got the carving fork and firmly spitted him to the board. The reptile coiled around her arm but she kept the head nailed through a roasting summer afternoon till her husband returned from work to rescue her. Every man's hand was so against the poor creatures that it would be said of a no-account character, "That fellow, he'd let a snake get away!"

Many women were courageous and adept in snake-killing and kept a snake-stick at hand. This was often a sucker, that had sprouted tough and supple from a stringybark or gum stump, with a knobby end to smash the delicately articulated spine of the snake. One of my aunts, finding herself in the entrance hall when a snake came to call, took the loaded shotgun which stood in the corner ready for

rchard or chicken marauders, and blew the intruder to
ieces on the hardwood floor and found it very like an
xploded fish. Even land snakes are good swimmers and
ndulate through the water with the same ease and grace
s on land. Once a hunted snake at Bobilla escaped past me
own a slope in such wide curves that he was almost
traight and seemed to be gliding a foot above the ground
vithout touching it.

Few snakes have been familiar. I have never had one in
ay hand, and could not bring myself to touch even a dead
ne. The only time I was touched by one was when hang-
ag some laundry on the line. I felt something rubbing
ound my stockinged legs lightly as my pussy was in the
abit of doing. I glanced down so as not to step on her and
aw a long fat leaden-coloured snake. I sprang away with a
creech that brought my father who was digging a bed in
ae flower garden. He killed the creature with his spade: "I
ever saw another snake act like it. It really seemed as if it
vanted to be friendly. It neither slithered away nor showed
ght. It seemed cowardly to kill the poor thing."

On one of those soft dark summer nights without moon
r stars in the sweet cool of the flat near the waterholes I
od on something the size of a hoe handle that was resili-
nt, and my foot thus rudely spoiled the snake's as well as
ay own sortie.

I had a lovely tabby cat adored by me and suffered by
Iother till she became a menace. I had smuggled her to bed
s a kitten, which was forbidden on the grounds of hygiene,
ut what child can resist the cuddlesome allurement of a
itten, or of a cat of any age?—the most seductive and
ouse-broken of all domestic animals, the only one who
an command complete social equality with man. Ning
oved the bush as much as I did. She took to roaming in it
nd to finding her own food there. She became a snake-
iller, whether for sport or sustenance, who can say? For

117

some time after reversion to type she would return through
the window before dawn for a snooze on the foot of my
bed. She occasionally saved a snake's head for me. We had
not guessed her proclivities till one morning I found the
abhorrent object on the mat beside my bed. Articles in the
papers had stated that the skeleton head of a snake could
retain poison in the fangs and if stepped on by bare feet
could have serious consequences. I would lie awake sick
with fear of Ning's approach lest when she inspected me
by putting her face so close to mine that her whisker
tickled me and I could feel her breathing, she might de
posit her odious trophy on me. I would close window
and door on sweltering nights for safety.

Three snakes have prominence in my memories of Ajin
by.

One day I chased a spotted butterfly to where it alighted
on the apple blossoms. I bounded through clumps of garden
escapes which contributed their share of colours—static
lupins, calliopsis, pincushions and many others. The orch
ard was in full bloom. An orchard so decked on a warm
spring day is a heaven of beauty and perfume. My grand
ma's was the most lovable orchard in the world, but it must
await a later paragraph. The snake has priority in this
At the foot of the great apple-tree a snake was coiled like a
whip with about a foot of the head upraised as straight as a
walking-stick. I fled wildly and said nothing of the incident
for I was supposed to be studying my lessons on the ver
anda. Still I can see that snake in its dangerous attitude
ready to strike. The only coiled snake in my experience
outside of a zoo.

One day later during my farewell sojourn in paradise
my youngest aunt yielded to my plea to go for a walk to
pick flowers. I had not outgrown the greedy desire of
children to grab flowers suffocatingly in their fists. No
native flower was then used in house decoration. Their elfin

118

ace could not compete in favour with the imported
ches of the garden plots. The cattle paddocks were bright
ith bloom, and, seeking variety, we followed one of our
viftly running home creeks, lovely as a fountain, through
veral fences to the hills. A big black snake lay full-length
his ease beside the water in the thin fringe of maidenhair
rns that were sprouting after winter retreat. The crea-
re's forked tongue flickered rapidly in and out, his new
in gleamed blue-black with peacock tints, a little of his
derside was showing like blended scarlet and pomegran-
e. I stood a fascinated moment and fled to my aunt. She
ent back seeking the snake but it had dissolved leaving
a trace.

The experience was not startling, merely surprising.
hen why should that snake have persisted in my conscious-
ss for over thirty years? As I have sat in some great
ngress in one of the major cities, or in a famous concert
ll, or eaten green almonds on a terrace in Turin in the
rly morning, or worked amid the din of the Krupp guns
a an Eastern battle front, or watched the albatrosses in
ormy weather off Cape Agulhas, or have been falling
leep in an attic in Bloomsbury, that snake has still been
retched in the ferns beside the creek, motionless except
r the darting tongue.

There came a day when the bone-ache for my birthplace
as being sunk in the rapture of return. It was the last time
was to see the old place in family ownership with my
cle and aunt and some of his family in residence. My
lored eldest maternal uncle (all my uncles were adored
d adorable, though some slightly more so than others)
d I were riding away from the homestead towards the
ur-mile gate. I reminded him how I had gone with him
ong that track on the occasion of a *first*. I was four and
had taken me for a ride for the first time without a
aring' rein. I remember the brown pony I rode—yes, a

119

pony for once, but she was quite thirteen hands, in fact smallish graceful horse, easy and trustworthy.

"Now, off I go and you follow!" said Uncle, breakir into a brisk canter. I was disrupted at being left behir instead of riding level, and demurred.

"Now, come on! You can't fall off. Cling like a spider cried Uncle. "We'll have a race."

Instantly I had a feeling of power and self-confidenc After that it was necessary to forbid me excessive speed.

I had reminded Uncle that a generation earlier, infar though I was, sartorial conventions had been strictly er forced. I then rode on a side-saddle with my small for from the waist down encased in an adult's riding skirt. was dark blue of some soft woollen material, a souven of my young aunt's governess. I felt noble and grand in as the little girls do today in suburban streets as the play at visiting in their mother's cast-off clothes. Short after this mother made me a habit of my own. It was black serge. It had a tidy squarecut jacket, braided, and th regulation skirt trimly to floor length, which had come in replace the long flowing Queen Victoria equestrian robe At the right side the skirt was enlarged for the knee go over the pommel or horn exactly like the smarte models for grown-ups. This had to be held up with th right hand when dismounted. I was such an exact replie of Mother that my appearance to take place on a ful sized horse never failed to excite astonished admiratio from strangers. On this later day I wore shirt and breech with top boots and sat astride.

I went doting and gloating on every rise and hollow that cherished way—that view where the river curves in wide bend confined by the hills that lean on the sky. Th voice of some mild rapids came from the distance. The Great-grandfather had first set his home. The funny o buzzard had disliked the river's symphonic song as t

oisy and moved farther up its banks to be quiet. I was
lling with healing nectar. I wanted to get away by myself
o indulge and savour emotions, releasing, relieving and
eyond communication. This view had nothing to out-
aatch dawn in the tropics, with the verdure and colour of
he volcanic islands rising above the ship, and the boom of
he combers on the coral, once heard never to be forgotten;
r the sky-line of New York challenging God and Nature
nd compelling obeisance from man, with the rising sun
etting the glass in its arrogant towers aflame; nor the satis-
action of the spires of Oxford, the Cambridge Backs, of
he dear familiar outlines of London filtered through racial
onsciousness since the Norman Conquest via our language
nd literature and direct parentage; nor the haunting myst-
ry of the Giant's Causeway and Glendalough; nor Paris
rresistibly enticing, nor that petrified austere majesty of the
Alps, of Rome, of Mt Olympus. Yes, they are all a part of
uman consciousness; but this obscure view had something
hat watered existence with the more intimate ecstasy of
ossession.

"Now," I announced, "I want to look at the creek where
aunt Alice and I walked when I was little and she a young
irl in her teens."

"There's no gate there now. You can't get on the home
rack again from that corner."

"All right. I'll just canter around and come back to
ou later."

I sought the spot where the snake had lain in my memory
or so long. The dense grove of the quick-growing brittle
cacia, with a broad leaf, that loves watery ground, was
one. Brambles and underbrush had been cleared away.
heep had succeeded the cattle and horses and cropped
verything close. The place was bare and flat and unrecog-
izable; the creek was stripped of its exquisite shrubs, but
: had not changed its course. That was the same as when

121

it had turned the mill put on it by some of the forebear
who otherwise had to grind wheat for their bread in :
quern in the evening when they desisted from felling and
grubbing and fencing to establish agriculture. But the spo
I sought was actively in my mind and the new rabbit-proo
fences followed the old lines so that I could be sure of it
And there was the snake! He lay in exactly the same posi
tion full-length in the sunlight on the right bank in the shor
grass, headed up-stream, motionless but for his forked
tongue. His blue-black coat glistened in the sun, his car
mined underside was partly discernible. It could have beer
the same creature lying there bewitched while I had travel
led in far places from infancy to middle age. I was smitten
to timelessness by something beyond my groping power
of expression. He lay supine. His fellow long ago had dis
appeared when I turned my back. I reined-in to conside
him. There was no coverage as of old, the stream wa
naked. I sat. I could have sat till the snake thought fit to
depart. But Uncle, having inspected a straying sheep, came
on to see what was detaining me. The snake did not depar
as I expected, as I had hoped. Uncle drew a girth from
his saddle and dismounted.

"Oh, Uncle! The poor creature! Let it go for old sake"
sake!"

"You must have gone soft in London among the Pom
mies and Yanks," he laughed, as he skilfully mangled th
snake.

"No, it's only that there was a snake there, in that posi
tion exactly, when I was tiny."

"You don't think it would be the same one waiting fo
you to come back!" remarked Uncle jovially. "Snakes ar
not travellers. You'll always find them or their progeny
in the same place year after year."

We rode away, I mourning the snake, and his ancestor o
long ago, which must now also be blasted from my con

sciousness, while Uncle related how he used to spring from his horse to seize a snake by the tail to break its back by cracking it like a whip. "I gave it up a few years ago when one came within a flash of getting me in the wrist. You lose your speed and suppleness after fifty."

On the following afternoon I rode alone along the old tracks to join Uncle and there in the same direction lying in the sun was another black snake to complete the trio. A lethal stick was handy. I was a little too timid physically to be worthy of my relatives and upbringing: I apologized to the snake for what had happened to his contemporary on the previous day and was relieved to leave him undisturbed in enjoyment of his native earth, which he perhaps was worthier to infest than I.

23

Uncle's goanna

IN VIEW of my horror of snakes I am inconsistently attached to lizards of various sizes and shapes. This predilection extends to tarantulas and spiders which I admire, and to Christmas beetles and cicadas which I enjoy clinging to my neck with their acute little claws.

Not far from Stillwater there were droves of what we called sleepy lizards. At least three to a panel of fencing could be seen dozing in the sun. What they lived on was a mystery though they were flycatchers and the flies covered everything. These lizards looked revolting enough for such a diet, but what alchemy made it so fattening? They bulged and hissed like those called the blue-tongued. The favourites of the species were the replicas of the goannas in a small size known as jew-lizards. Why jew, and why jew-lizard frill was never clear. At this distance a Presbyterian frill would seem more descriptive, remembering the number of shaven lips and chins with a disfiguring rim of beard around them to be seen on pictures of gentlemen of that persuasion.

The jew-lizards were brave and hardy and harmless. Boys

ept them in their pockets to annoy little girls and for other purposes, not often kind, you may be sure. One of my brothers had a pet that sat on a block every morning while he milked the cows. He had first squirted milk on it for mischief, but the creature licked-in the fluid with relish. After that it would open its mouth while my brother accurately directed the milk and gurgled with glee and pride. No other boy had such a lizard.

There were smooth clayey tracks in this part of the country in which in the mornings we found the cavities scooped by the lizards for their eggs. Carefully marked, the places could be found again later, and the eggs, small, whitish and leathery, unearthed and smashed. No one ever thought of the lizards' side of it.

When we were not too busy collecting the delicious manna dropped by the brittle or manna gums of the region we would be swimming in the weedy waterholes with the small fresh-water tortoises. Sometimes they would collide with us. We caught them to take home for pets. Mother forbade this as cruelty. Father wondered what could be the matter with the tortoises that we could catch them with our hands. Later scores of their carapaces lined the banks of the waterholes, though the nature of the illness was undetermined.

To companion the tortoises were leeches galore. There was no sale for them or the boys could have earned pocket money. My brothers and their mates competed to see who could have the most of these odious suckers on their bodies at the one time. Boys crave the gruesome and cruel. These had revolting patches of sores from the suction but they were not found out because young and old covered their bodies. The proprieties were strictly observed. The boys swam naked in one hole and I had to wear a singlet and a pair of drawers in another just out of sight. Sometimes my favourite brother, to indulge me, would leave on his knee-length trousers and give me a few lessons secretly i the boys' hole, show me how to take off in a dive from treasured rock. Rocks were rare there.

At Ajinby there was a heavenly swimming-hole in th creek below some miniature rapids and a tiny fall. Th warm rocks were like tables on the bank. The glory o teatree, blackthorn and other shrubs with the ever-presen maidenhair and mimulus were all about. The platypuse sported with us. We had tins of worms, tiny fish-hooks— sometimes only bent pins—on twine and wattle saplin and fished for the small speckled indigenous trout calle slipperies. These were also in the waterholes at Stillwate and sometimes at picnics we'd take a pan and fry the fresh. The sweetest fish ever tasted disappeared before th drier, larger, greedier, imported rainbow trout. Gone als is much of the unique shrubbery of the streams so that me can swirl expensive lines and artificial flies in some sort c fishing ritual analogous to fox-hunting. It was my younges uncle, with me looking on, who first let loose in thos streams the invaders that came tiny as tadpoles in mill cans from government hatcheries.

At Ajinby the men swam in a bigger, more dangerou place in the river where the creek joined it. With us the were the goannas of the smaller water species which scu tled away, ludicrous as they lifted their long tails like startled old lady of a bygone regime grabbing her skir to show white stockings and elastic-sided boots.

The goanna was the King Billy of lizards. We stood little in awe of the big grey fellows. They had the reputa tion of biting attacking dogs, and blood-poisoning wa feared from the goanna's habit of eating carrion. Goanna enjoyed the favour of men. Men enjoyed them as they di smokingroom jokes and usually chuckled when telling stor ies of them. When chased they take to a tree and keep th trunk between themselves and the enemy. We woul

ochre them by surrounding the tree, when the wily strat-
gist would climb to a high horizontal branch and put it
between himself and us. They were privileged because they
were entertaining, living things in the paddocks and later
were protected by law because they eat rabbits.

My uncle had a goanna that grew too bumptious. She
was a gourmand with an appetite for hen's eggs. There
were plenty of them, to be sure. This uncle, who had early
carried me on the purple pillow, made a married home in
another part of the country. His flocks were of first class
merinos, his fowls well-bred Orpingtons, Plymouth Rocks
or other sizeable and stable breeds. One big goanna preferred the eggs warm from the hens to all other diets and
had an unwieldy appetite. The terrified hens betrayed her.
Aunt objected to their being frightened away to lay in the
paddocks for the foxes. Goanna had been chased away a
mile or more several times but speedily returned. The time
came to exile her at the farthest part of the sheep run miles
away. All those old enough to ride saddled their horses and
prepared long switches with a bunch of twigs on the end.
Uncle chose a mare who could be relied upon not to panic.
He and the jackeroo each put a rope on goanna, which
took finesse. The dogs were delirious to join the party
but were safely chained. There was no guarantee that they
would confine their nips to "heeling" when they had such a
challenging adversary helpless, and goanna was not to be
injured or humiliated. Uncle and the jackeroo mounted,
each with a rope so that they could prevent goanna from
ascending the horses, an outrage to give them hysterics. As
it was they were inclined to rear and gallop, but the guy
ropes kept goanna from touching them. She was excited
and rampageous and protested in a sort of *wuth-wuthing*
between a hiss and a bark which resulted in the regurgita-
tion of a whole clutch of purloined eggs still unbroken.

This was greeted with laughter. "The greedy old scound-

rel! She can't say she didn't do it!" Uncle laughed indul
gently. "She's a champion all right!"

One of us rode ahead to have the gates wide oper
Others kept in the rear to tickle goanna when she jibbec
We left her up a tree unhurt and defiant. The jolly outin
ended in morning tea with oodles of rich cakelets fres
from the oven on the wide trellised verandas where Aunti
listened to the tale of goanna's antics—all in the old Aus
tralian way of life now being erased by the New Age.

24

Grandma's orchard

THE diminishing weeks were frantically savoured. I ran hither and yon as intensely as a dog left in charge, trying to garner concretely the intangible. The beauty of the orchard in bloom had excited me as an ethereal wonderland. Those heralds, the peach-trees, had been everywhere, almost unregarded, patches of rose amid the native foliage along the race or creeks where their pits had been dropped to make fruit for the possums. The pear, the plum and the cherry-trees were ladies-in-waiting. The quince with her quieter blooms was a handmaiden. The great apple-tree stood like the queen of them all in her pastel rosiness with her promise of substantial gifts to last through the bare months. Her bridal radiance was overwhelming under the fresh warm spring skies. The butterflies paid her court in flickering beauty spots of added adornment.

The cherries ripened first and disappeared quickly. The leatherheads chanting *cholicky-cholicky* sensed their arrival from afar: only sharp-shooting saved for us some of the black and white-heart beauties grown on trees grafted by Great-uncle William himself. He was a skilled orchardist and agriculturist, one of the ablest pupils of Calloway. Fruit-trees were respected and loved. There was no hacking them to let the riflers or sprayers have easy access. Each tree was a personality like members of the family themselves. When pruned the superfluous limbs were carefully selected, sawn with a surgeon's amputating precision and then plastered with mud lest the powerful Australian sun should prove fatal. Each tree was allowed to develop grandly to its full height and to live to its full age. They responded by bearing nobly for generations.

Another early treat were the apricots on a tall tree that guarded the back gate and threw shade where Grandma had made the splendid swipe at me with the broom. I held an idea that five pips were the correct number for an apple. Mother told us of her grandmother on a visit bringing a beautiful apple, one of several that had come all the way from Prospect by bullock dray. Each one had enjoyed a taste of it and its five pips were saved for increase. Two trees resulted. These were, I believe, the queen already mentioned, and another that stood not far away among the oldest trees near the house. The queen's fruit was large and green. They turned yellow only when ripe. The flesh juicy when newly ripe, delicious for eating raw or cooking, would mellow to dry flour that could be scooped out with a spoon. When ripe their broad flatness allowed them to be split in halves by hand. The second tree was not so tall and had less massive limbs. The fruit was small. We called the apples "russets" because they had a tough brown skin. The flesh was yellow with a nutty flavour. Both these apples would remain in the straw in the loft where they were carefully placed till the second season's early fruits would be well advanced. The straw seemed to suck the flavour from the big apples, but the hardy russets retained theirs and were much prized when there was no cold storage, no exchange of fruits from afar. There was

130

so the earliest apple, the Irish peach or the Dunlop, small ples with dark speckled skins. At the head Bobilla home- ead too and other haunts of my childhood were numerous nnamed seedling apples equally remarkable. There was no sease, no codlin moth, fruit flies, nor the most insidious of , the brown rot which was to be seen destroying even ing George V's peaches exhibited at the Chelsea Flower ow.

Gathering the apples for winter was a pleasant and satis- ing task. The fruit was allowed to ripen to the right gree to retain its full flavour. It was not plucked so green at it never ripened or ripened so unnaturally that the vour was spoiled. Uncles would ascend the great trees choose the best apples for eating raw. These were tossed my aunts to be placed tenderly in the big laundry bask- s. My youngest aunt could catch like a cricket fielder. ny apple with a bruise or blemish was rejected. Then me the fuller harvest in various grades, not quite so ecially handled but nevertheless sorted and laid on shelves. here were hundredweights in addition that could be eaten day. The residue fell on the ground and was a tasty ssert for the pigs.

In a corner outside the flower garden was the domain the gooseberries, the red and white currants and the spberries. A tall magnolia looked over the flower-garden nce to watch my foraging and feasting.

Thickets of Kentish cherries yielded appetizing fruit es- cially delicious for preserves. The pigs crushed their nes with gusto which, seeing how their teeth are placed, ways seemed clever marksmanship to me. Peaches were entiful. Luscious pears that would melt in the mouth, d others so hardy that they lasted till spring and so eighty that a couple could serve a family, were a treat, ked in the brick oven with cloves stuck in them. The inces, never to be outgrown in affection, would hang

131

like yellow lanterns on the trees after the leaves ha
fallen, the most lasting of the orchard's bounty and no
more appetizing stewed or baked or in pies with clott
cream or preserved in jellies and jams.

Among such riches none was more plentiful, more varie
more luscious than the plums. Strange fruit, among t
sweetest raw, among the sourest cooked. I don't know the
species but in the gardens of my childhood I can clear
recall eighteen different kinds. Sometimes in the night wh
sleep will not come I summon them to mind. A small swe
one called the American came first. Also early and one
the choicest was the greengage. There followed the purp
and the red, oval or round, large and small, including t
big Victoria, and one of the handsomest called the Ja
anese, which was untameably sour, raw or cooked. It w
delightful to shake a tree or to hit it with a prop-stick f
the ripest fruit to fall. Plums were with us for the fu
season right through to autumn with the white and purp
prunes, the big whitish floury egg plums, then the sm
roundish damson plum and the oval damson herself. T
damson is the beloved of those reared in the cold countr
When truly ripe, stewed with its royally coloured juic
served with plenty of thick scalded cream it is a dish f
epicures. And a damson-tree laden with ripening fr
thrills with its dark beauty. The rarest, most tribal plu
of all was the gizzard plum. It lasted longest of any a
shared with the prunes the honour of best for drying.
was smallish, the size of the damson plum, with the halv
plainly indented. Unless quite ripe it was astringent a
puckered the lips. Properly ripe it vies with the damson
memory. Dried it turned dark and leathery like the coo
ed gizzard of a hen, but in pies, with thick cream again,
and the damson had the winter to themselves.

I never saw a gizzard plum anywhere but in Grandm
orchard, and two immense old trees farther up the riv

in some spot which had been the home plot of a settler long gone. We thought that "gizzard" was our private name for it, and Grandma did not consider it quite genteel to call it that to topside guests.

One day long after on Tottenham Court Road not far from Oxford Street I was turning over the wares on the pavement outside Shearn's, the well-known fruiterer. A shop assistant brought me to heel with, "Can I help you to find something, Madam?"

"I was looking for gizzard plums," I mumbled.

"Ask at the counter inside, Madam; fourpence per pound."

A pound of fruit in a bag was quickly in my hand. I stuck in my thumb and pulled out a plum, and thoroughly dumbfounded was I. It was ripe and sweet, of rare flavour, unmistakably a *Gizzard Plum*! ! !

I sallied out dazed, never more integrally of the British Empire.

My Queensland friend, she who caressed the carpet-snake, and had inherited a prejudice against the English, laughed merrily,

"Yes! There's no doubt they are the most remarkable people on the globe. I wouldn't believe it with their stick-in-mud tinpot ways and all that broken glass on top of their old walls to keep people out, but one day at Kew I found in a hothouse a pot full of our old sourgrass weed that grows round the stables at home!"

25

The chicken

ASSIDUITY in accumulation of feminine accomplishments would have made my tendencies less disturbing but much as I loved every cranny of the old house, and able though I was in duties there I relegated them to secondary importance. To perch on top of a post to watch the drafting at the yards or the wool-pressing, to be placed somewhere else in safety while old Simon, the dear, faithful bob-tailed horse, trod the rounds in chaff-cutting—many such enterprises during my liberty to roam about with my uncles may have engendered the attitude of leaving the house to the women. It was certainly easier to sit on a pedestal while the men laboured in my sight than myself to labour as underling to my female elders.

Practice in household occupations from infancy, and natural quickness, made them easy, but to despatch them was not enough in the feminine sphere. There must be no other preoccupation for a girl. Her mind must not probe beyond limits tacitly understood.

The domestic arts can be absorbing. They are basic for decent, comfortable life as organized by men for centuries.

out to be discouraged in the realm of mental speculation till the mind becomes inelastic and atrophied was what I subconsciously resisted. I strove to evade the oncoming doom of contraction to the housewife's hen-mindedness, or incarceration in her cage by escape into nature.

Beyond the orchard was a tiny paddock of two acres for the horses of overnight guests and the night horse—some swift and reliable beast, the forerunner of the telephone. Spread upward from this and the orchard was a larger paddock of sixty acres for the cows and, when in use, the working bullocks. On the other side were oat and wheat, potato and pumpkin paddocks, and sheep and horse runs. These led to the four-mile gate and beyond in the direction intersected by the creek beside which the snake had recently been seen, and thence upward to the wild hills, the domain of brumbies and clean-skin cattle. I loved the cow paddock. It had been cleared by hand by two of my uncles as lads, of great trees and underscrub so thick that a dog could not bark in it, to use the local phrase. It stretched to the foothills of the high ranges. From the top end there was now a clear view down the long slope. One could descry what was afoot (influence of Walter Scott) about the premises: who was coming in, going out, or passing on the Monaro road beside the creek. Up there the turkeys roamed and nested slyly, as their habit is. It was delight to find their eggs in gum-leaves half-dried and tangy of boughs left from a young tree recently felled for a long rail or post. The eggs were half-hidden by leaves among the long fine silky drying grasses. The turkey hen preserves the artistry and cunning of untamed birds. The eggs, covered with tan freckles and more pointed than those of other domesticated fowls, are small compared with the size of the layer, and the most delicate of all to eat softboiled in the shell.

The turkeys were among Grandma's diversions. "I can't

find that turkey's nest. She will be coming home with a brood too late in the season to thrive," she observed.

"I've got her nest at the very top of the cow paddock."

"When were you at the top of the cow paddock? Who was with you?"

"No one. I was up there just before dinner."

"I left you doing your lessons on the veranda."

"But I finished them long ago."

That was the trouble. No one knew enough to train me in higher arithmetic. I could learn all the allotted tables of weights and measurements in a twinkling. I revelled in the old spelling book and absorbed pages of words in the time allotted to master a column. Everyone was tired of examining my prowess in that line. There was not enough talent in the teachers to make the piano interesting. I would go through the five-finger exercises and scales and then make up more of my own. This strumming could be heard and was forbidden. Sometimes I am reminded of my efforts by "modern" music over the radio.

"Running about like a gipsy," said Grandma. "You might get bitten by a snake or come to other harm. The swagmen camp up there."

"They wouldn't hurt me. They always say 'Gooday Missy.'"

"It's hopeless trying to make you genteel. School with your brothers and sisters is the only place for you, my lady! Children of your own age will put you in your place. Such a big girl now, you should be ashamed of yourself to be running about idle like a boy."

Nothing more was said in my hearing. A firm rule in my family was never to discuss children in their presence either in praise or blame. Divided authority was avoided. A rebuke was between the culprit and the rebuker. It was never carried over. That would have been nagging and ungenteel. Sulks or vindictiveness were accounted sin by

Grandma: "'Vengeance is mine, I will repay,' saith the Lord." Discipline was firm but not tyrannous. It was applied as a scaffolding or mould till it became self-applied in self-control and abstemiousness.

In my brief sortie into the other world of Stillwater I had met a girl of my own age with a violent temper which she would reinforce with black sulks. Everyone bowed to her. She took what she wanted from us young folks. I envied such power. One day I was moved to actual emulation. Grandma had corrected me for some fault or other. I remember only that I resented that she had cast me out of her favour, and on this day was talking to me as usual without having "made it up". I gathered my face together and walked away from her. My uncle, meeting me, asked, "What's the matter with you? You have a lip like a motherless foal."

Each time I approached Grandma I scowled and glared till at last she was forced to observe. "What are you looking like that for? A dose of senna tea might do you good. What have you been eating?"

I hung my head in imitation of my admired model and glowered more intensely, though the unfamiliar rôle was difficult. My antics aroused Grandma.

"You look as if you are sickening for something. Perhaps a dose of castor oil would be better than the senna."

"Yesterday you said you could not put up with me. You said there was no use in me pretending to be friendly, and today you . . ."

Grandma broke into her merry laughter and took hold of me, excruciatingly amused. "So you are not friends with your old Grannie because she was cross with you yesterday! I have forgotten all about that long ago." She tickled me as gaily as if she had been a young girl and instilled an abomination of sulks, etc. I have never felt sulky naturally. That was the only time I ever attempted to assume sulks.

137

I had the joy of taking Grandma for exercise to the top of the cow paddock to the turkey's nest. She broke one of the eggs and found that the chicks were so far along that she would have to let them come out. She promised that I could feed them. I could run up to keep watch for their arrival to outstrip the crows, but must always say when I was going and come straight back. "And to try to be more genteel, to please your Grannie."

I promised. Thus full freedom to roam in one part of the outdoors was curtailed.

I studied at a table on the coolest end of the veranda where a wistaria vine luxuriated and the Parramatta rose and little-girl box-tree held guard. It had been convenient and tempting to steal past the passion flower, the pomegranate, the bignonia and the sentinel magnolia to a secluded gate, thence by a little bridge over a big drain to fill my stomach with gooseberries, and then behind shrubs and trees to a quince-tree, whose limbs took me to the top of the palings. From these I elongated into the cow paddock. Now when I had finished my lessons and wished to evade some confining task I tiptoed the other way to the horticultural nursery garden, where bloomed a splendid shrub of *prostanthera* set by my mother, to the schoolhouse and the famous orange-tree, thence along a path to a side gate under a spreading fig-tree whose branches I would later climb to gorge on the fruit. Out past the great willow-tree and Grandma's vegetable garden by the buggy-house and dray-sheds, the blacksmith's shop, leaving the woodpile and gallows on the left; out of the big back yard by a gate that led to a lucerne field and a delicious path up a slope across the race to the woolshed, the shearers' hut and an extended and exciting beyond. I stayed near at hand today. Here was the working man's comfortable two-roomed hut. The white clover was deep and green all about. Here and there was a fruit-tree sprung from some carelessly hrown pip, heavily laden with ripening treasure and lending a park-like aspect. The fowlhouse opened on to this domain where had lurked fleas and ringworms.

Today I craved the company of a nice fat chicken, not yet feathered, irresistible as are all young furred and feathered creatures. The chicks clustered about me, it seemed so easy to catch one, but the hen suspected me and warned them excitedly, and the clover hid them. I threw myself where one seemed to have disappeared. I detained the chicken all right but the soft warm body was limp in my hand. It was dead! I felt like Cain. My recently abrogated subervience to God and his all-watchful eye, even of fallen sparrows, revived. It was a dreadful feeling. The hen moved away, fussily cluck-clucking her family to safety. I sat in the blossoming clover thick with bees and butterflies, the crime in my hand to make the warm sunlight chilly and the river lullaby sound as intrusively as it did before a storm.

As I sat pondering the burial of the chicken, the vulnerable body moved in my hand. The relief of that moment with its release from a sense of sin can never be forgotten. The working man, coming from the stockyards, found me.

"What's the matter with the chicken? Where's the old hen?"

He took the chick from my hand.

"Poor little beggar! Chicken-hawk or one of the pups must have got at it. Its beak is busted right off. It's no more good. I'll wring its neck."

This galvanized me to grasp the chicken with the intensity of a mother with a defective child. Surely enough the lower half of the bill was broken clean off, the result of my attack.

"He won't be able to eat a bite. He'll starve in a day or two. Save him a lot of trouble to wring his neck now."

"He won't starve. I'll feed him."

"Ha! Ha! You'll soon get tired of that."

"I won't! Besides, how do you know it's a *he*?"

"Whichever he is it won't put his beak on again."

I released the chicken to its family and at feeding time was a helpful little girl and took charge. The chicken put its half beak on the food helplessly. It was easily caught this time. I stuffed it full of pellets of pollard and gave it a drink by pouring two teaspoonfuls of water down its throat.

The working man forgot about the mutilated chicken. Deaths among larger animals were familiar, the loss of a chick was no more than a flick. Grandma did not notice the chicken for a while, not till one of the deepest of human needs drove me to an audience. She was warmly interested and warned me against neglect. No need. I have been burdened always with too much affection for people, places and things. Passionate love of relatives, of friends, of the ranges, the streams, the trees, horses, cats, of the beauty in the dawns and sunsets and starry nights—a multitude of experiences that other people take more mildly.

Grandma and uncles became interested in my unwavering devotion to the chicken. I stuck to its feeding and watering so that it out-stripped its family in sleek health. I would not leave the premises unless Grandma undertook its care in my stead. This compensated for my contempt for dolls and my indifference to companions younger than myself. I became addicted to babies and toddlers only in my mid-teens when they dropped into their own special class as young things. My present attitude was the result of their inanity, and resentment of it when segregated in their company, while the chicken was an object of infatuation because its helplessness and dependence on me gratified another human desire.

In light of early forwardness I was singularly reluctant

to progress farther. The precocities or any charms of the tiny tot had vanished in the unattractive stage of a big girl, though one still a child, lost without the family. I loved the old nest with maturing passion, the mountains and hills, its rivers and creeks, its rocks and paddocks, though I could no longer roam about even the nearer precincts without accounting for my time, nor accompany the men farther afield.

The limitations of the company of infants and toddlers now confronted me again in restriction to the women's domain. The artificial bonds called feminine were presented to my understanding. I must become genteel as befitting a young lady. A good deal was attributed to God's will, and did not turn my heart any more warmly to that gentleman. It was the humbug in "womanliness", the distorting and atrophying of minds on a sex line, the grinding superstition that all women must be activated on a more or less moronic level, the absence of fair play between men and women when the masculine and feminine issue arose that was at the root of the trouble, though I did not know so much in my first decade. I was more bewildered and tormented and rebellious in my second, when preoccupation with sex was discovered to be in excess of all needs for perpetuating the species, and banished logic from human behaviour.

For the present I was merely a froward girl and had to be curbed for my own good. Grandma alone used the word froward, which I took as her pronunciation of "forward". The word was familiar in the Bible, but the Bible's vocabulary was something apart like men's second set of manners for women of a special class. To me "froward" meant a bold hussy—deep degradation in disapproval. It was an aspersion I never merited and as I grew to understand all that I imagined the word connoted it festered slightly in my heart. Half a lifetime later I came across the word in the dictionary and realized my mistake with a sense of reprieve from a slur.

Grandma would look over her specs to say, "Your froward heart will bring you trouble. You must pray to God to cure you of it."

It was the exact word, and Grandma's prophecy was to come true in much heart-burning.

Grandma still respected me for my truthfulness and certain other qualities, but when she went to prepare the fruits for the Christmas cakes and puddings the raisins had sadly diminished. I was suspected. I had not known where the raisins were kept, and in any case would have had no temptation to take anything so sacrosanct. In spite of a lifetime of truthfulness Grandma did not this time believe me. The froward heart accounted for the deterioration. Grandma did not run to complex analysis.

"High time you were at school, my lady! This shows it. You must get away after Christmas in time to begin after the holidays."

Higher criticism of the Bible and a breach in truthfulness made me more uncomfortably an outcast than the ringworms. They had been partly an Act of God. Now I had broken the eighth commandment and told a lie. It was clear that school would put me in my place with people of my own age, where I would find it unbearable to be out of step with the feminine regiment.

Truth-telling, for which I was noted and which stood tremendous wear and tear before it began to have threadbare patches, was not—I have come to feel through adult self-analysis—due so much to virtue as to exceptional gifts of observation, supported by a turn for clear and accurate reporting. I revelled in exercising my faculties and was contemptuous of noodles who could not see exactly what had happened and how. To tell a thing straight was part of a love of order. Failure to do so was irritating to me.

"She was so truthful as a little thing," said Aunt M.

"When they get out with other children they soon learn evil. It changes them altogether," added Aunt A.

Alas, that pooling of childish knowledge should increase only evil!

Grandma said no further word to me of my sin, though I overheard her remarking to the mailman when instructing him to bring a fresh supply of raisins, "Young puss, she ate pounds of them, and refuses to admit it!"

I asserted over and over again that I did not commit this theft, but Grandma would not believe. I was bewildered as when struggling in a bad dream. The situation had some of the elements of Mrs M'G.'s misrepresentations but I could not clarify it. After Christmas the problem of this change in my character was to be passed on to my parents.

The shadow soon lifted. Louisa, the maid, confessed that she alone had pilfered the raisins. The blame had been firmly fixed without any punishment to wring her heart on my behalf. I was more perplexed than unhappy because of the accusation. Why was she moved to exonerate me and lower her own status? It was very handsome of her. I recall her with affection and admiration because of it. Her home life had not been so cosy as mine. Her family lacked prestige. She was considered sly. She had not been reared to outspokenness by self-assured individualists. Her mother was isolated in dense scrub far from neighbours and suffered so from her father that she appealed to the Governor of the State. He sent the local sergeant of police to investigate. The upshot was a divorce. This was a performance then confined to high society, and not without obloquy there. It was unheard-of in Louisa's world. Her mother became notorious as a subject of ridicule and astonishment throughout Monaro and beyond.

Louisa's fall from rectitude was treated with the same reticence and decorum as when it had been mine. It was never mentioned in my hearing. To throw up to anyone a past misdemeanour or anything derogatory would have been to descend to the level of those who billingsgated.

My character was restored but not cleansed of frowardness. The slogan that I must go home to be a help to my mother, etc., etc., after Christmas, did not wane.

26

After Christmas

NOTHING could now hold back my departure, nothing but Christmas. That Christmas, partly a bulwark, partly a bugbear, had left few memories. It was a bugbear because after Christmas I was to leave Ajinby indefinitely, and when one is ten that means eternity. After Christmas! *After Christmas!*

Christmas was the frail barrier that stood between me and exile. I had till after Christmas! After Christmas!

Among the guests that Christmas there would be two to succeed me. One was the infant son of my elder aunt, who would come to her old home with him for his first Christmas under the family roof.

I was more unremitting in attention to my chicken than to five-finger exercises on the piano. My young aunt as inducement to keep to them was coaching me in a light "piece", a little polka in which I should surprise the household as a pianist. The day came. Aunts and Grandma with the visiting aunt and son, assembled in the drawingroom and sat politely ready for the ordeal. The new grandson was laid on a rug on the floor to be cool. Full of importance

I began, and was getting on as well as could be expected when the infant rolled over and began to crawl for the first time. Great excitement! but I kept on with the "piece". I could feel my audience losing interest in me as exclamations rose behind me. My heart sank in disappointment, but the determination to get to the end as a matter of tidiness like the clear reporting, was innate. I finished. I had made no mistake, had not thumped or gone too quickly, I expected commendation. Not a word. All were engrossed in the infant's performance. No, not all. My Aunt Metta sat on the sofa as attentively and elegantly upright as when I had started. She said in her soft gracious voice, "Thank you, Stella," as if she meant it, in exactly the tone and words she would have employed to an adult.

Joy and warmth returned. Her influence is to be gauged by the many times since then I have waited with sympathy and simulated appreciation to thank some other child or indifferent performer being similarly neglected. The lack of interest in my performance at least armoured me against expectation of adulation or of being deceived by it as anything more than politeness should it occur.

The second successor was a granddaughter of three, an enchanting wee person who came for the annual gathering with my eldest maternal uncle and her mother.

Our parents did not believe in children living on cakes or sweets, nor in eating at odd hours. When we were grown, three good meals a day and dry bread between was my mother's sound rule against "stuffing". If we were hungry we would enjoy the bread, said she. I don't recall even the boys, who yelped most loudly about their appetites *alias* hunger, ever having had recourse to the dry bread.

Mother served us at meals without consulting our preferences or whims. Christmas midday dinner was an exception. Then each according to age was allowed to express a preference. This Christmas, Ruby in the high chair, and I, were the two youngest, excluding the baby, who was on milk diet. Uncle sat in Grandma's place at the head of the table and carved. Ruby's turn came.

"Ruby, what would you prefer?"

The baby pipe was clear. "Please Father, I'll have some veg-ee-tatables."

As was the family custom, her vocabulary was without baby pidgin and she conquered the long word by emphasis. Uncle was as grave and polite as Aunt Metta after my solo.

"Yes, but what would you like with the vegetables?" The little girl hung to the vegetables, so Uncle said, "I think you would enjoy a bit of breast and some seasoning with the vegetables."

This incident was to be reproduced at Stillwater when my little sister in her turn had reached Ruby's age and it was Christmas. She too was in her high chair and the last on the list. "Laurel, what can I help you to?" proceeded Father in grave ritual.

"Please, Father, I'll have fum sowl" (some fowl).

In the excitement of choice she had changed the initial letters. It stuck in my mind because she knew no goo-goo patter. Mother held that a child had enough to learn without being clogged by silly affectations that had later to be dropped. This made another gap in my training so that I cannot talk to children except as adults in embryo, careful of their dignity. As it had been an entertainment for my seniors in my infancy to tutor me in a sesquipedalian vocabulary, so we continued among ourselves, and Laurel, the final baby, was our pride. On a visit to Grandma and aunts when she was three, one aunt inquired, "Did you come on the puff-puff?"

The child looked slightly puzzled and then asked, "Do you mean the locomotive engine?"

"This one seems to be even more prodigious than the

others," laughed the aunts. The child had time to prove it before she died at eleven.

Christmas past, there was comparative relaxation compared with the bustle and anticipation of preparation. The beef cask was supplied, the bins full, cake tins packed with biscuits in rich variety, and not one but many Christmas cakes and puddings awaited their turn. The cool earthen floor of a pantry for preserves was crowded with bottles of home-made beers and cordials. Eggs were as plentiful as peas. The vegetable garden and orchards were heavy with spoils.

In the days before swift transport the custom was for the separate families of a clan each to gather in its own nest for Christmas day. Following that was a period of inter-visiting. Visitors stayed for a night, a week, or a month. Among those that came were two girls a little my senior, the delightful E., and L., my aunts' young cousin. It seemed to me that all ingenuity and social knowledge were centred in them. They enjoyed themselves in a variety of ways that had never occurred to me, restricted to the sobriety of elders. I worshipped them thereafter. They were a first experience of youthful companions who could be exhilarating.

The work of keeping the home running so smoothly was prodigious but to take part in it was entertainment. Portly men in kitchen aprons took charge of washing the dishes, lanky young cavaliers in long spurs waved tea-towels. Others purloined my aunts' sunbonnets as badges of office and found usefulness. It was like a pantomime charade run for spontaneous zest in living and pleasure in association. Jokes and quips flew.

Even uninvited or uninviting guests never knew tired table- or bed-linen in the homes of Grandma or Mother. The washing equalled that of a public house. The laundry stood in the inner back yard. It had the usual big fireplace

or the boiling, many tubs of all sizes—some wooden—a
amping-down table, a slab for the scrubbing of working
oleskins, and baskets big enough to hold Falstaff and
mall enough to cradle Moses. The washing-machine was a
ecies of cradle swung on a stand, and took two to rock
. This chore was generally the refuge and wonderment
f the untrained men visitors from overseas. This delectable
partment was shaded by a giant mulberry-tree, and out-
de the back window in the embrasure of the fireplace was
Grandma's latest pet, a young loquat-tree.

I led the two cousins of my age bracket to the roof of
e wash-house. There we could lie in the shade of the
ulberry and gorge on its fruit or pick enough for pies to
e eaten with clotted cream. The visitors prevailed upon
y youngest aunt to reach up a fishing line and a small
asket by which we sent down choice mulberries and in
turn she passed up ginger beer and cake. Oh, those cakes,
ade with no stringencies in eggs or butter!

Spring water was pumped from a well near the laundry
d carried by spouting to two big casks. One stood beside
e kitchen door, the other in the laundry. Drinking water
as always pumped fresh from the well. Grandma decreed
at the casks must always be kept full in case of fire, and
keep the casks tight. The pumping was entrusted to the
ung fry with me as the leader. The sentinel failed in
r watch at the filling cask with the result of flooding.
randma forbade water fights as ruffianly, though nothing
more natural to young people when the weather is hot.
n this occasion guests not so genteel were tempted when
earing up the flood, and the chasing and laughing and
pping were on. A glance from Grandma kept me to heel
a young man from Sydney evidently did not like the
n. A stranger, he did not fully realize that Grandma was
verenced like Queen Victoria, and dived into her bed-
om where no man entered lightly, not even uncles. He

was safe from followers, but Grandma herself becam[e]
infected with the spirit of the chase or resented the youn[g]
man's temerity in seeking such a refuge. She handed me [a]
dipper of water and said, "After him! After him! He wen[t]
in the side door."

While the hunters ignored him I sped to Grandma's room
where, sure enough, the culprit was crawling under he[r]
curtained double bed with a discreet valance around [it]
right to the floor. Normally he would have been safe ti[ll]
the rumpus subsided but I caught him right on the fac[e]
and chest. Why Grandma relaxed gentility and risked de[-]
bauching me I cannot tell, but 'twas a glorious victory.

27

Exit from Eden

EVERYTHING became more precious to my passionately doting heart as departure drew near. This included the chicken. He was now a sizeable bird under my unremitting care and an object of interest to all. His possession had given me prestige among the visiting children. People would inquire after him and linger to see him fed.

"It's amusing to see him open his mouth for the water."

He was my treasure.

"Who's going to look after the chicken when you leave him?"

"If you could stay a few weeks longer he would be fit for the pot." The person who made this horrifying suggestion was ruled out as dangerous.

"You'll have to take your chicken with you."

This I had determined to do. I would have carried him tucked under my arm, which seemed easy and reasonable to me.

My loveliest of relatives, Aunt Metta, was to escort me to my parents. She was considered beautiful with her skin like alabaster and the almost colourless eyes of the peoples

151

of the extreme European north. Ribald youth at the teasing stage called them "sheep's eyes" but they gave her an unearthly delicacy like a painted angel. She spoke quietly in a low voice that she had difficulty in raising, so that she was exempt from roughening it by reading or reporting to Grandma, who was increasingly hard of hearing. She was one of the quietest members of the clan but that quietness contained nothing of meekness.

I worshipped her as perfect. She was as gifted with children as Aunt Lizzie or Uncle Hil and her charm was not confined to the under-tens. She was equally understanding of and beloved by adolescents, and had remained an ideal. She could correct or train me so sensitively that I was never wounded or resentful. When it was necessary to point out a flaw in manners or a mistake in conduct it remained between her and me. She was never to be overheard saying to Grandma, "She's so-and-so or such-and-such, you should speak to her," a procedure as normal as infuriating to youthful transgressors. I never knew her to lapse in good taste or integrity. Her severest rebuke was when I was nearly ten.

"I shall have to call you Miss Pert if you behave like that."

I was subdued instantly.

She had a delicately satirical sense of humour that was not sharp enough for the target to resent the shaft. Her sallies among louder tones would float past unheeded except by any with a sense of humour as penetrating as her own. A letter from her could be half the length of others but contain sap in every observation for those with the requisite apperceptiveness.

When departure drew near and I still talked with surety of taking the chicken I was surprised to hear her voice say, "Nonsense! It is not to be thought of!"

She was to deliver me and go on to Sydney for a holiday.

152

hich was a rare escape from the bush. I was an incumrance: a fowl crate was unthinkable.

"Why would it be nonsense, Auntie?"

"We mightn't get a porter when changing trains."

"I can easily carry him myself."

"How would you feed the creature on the way? It would
e of thirst."

"I could easily soak cake in tea for it."

"A nice spectacle you'd be with your good clothes plasted with cake, and smelling of the fowlhouse."

"I wouldn't! I'd wear my pinafore."

A noble concession this. I was to wear one of the sumer dresses my aunts had made me without a pinafore, that ork-a-day badge of childhood.

"I refuse to take a fowl crate," said Aunt Metta firmly.

So grievous was the thought of separation from that soft uggling form that I'd hold him in my arms and dream up ntasies to meet the situation.

"Grandma, I could put him in a box, couldn't I?" Granda was more intimate with my intimacy with the bird and rhaps better understood my devotion than anyone else. lso it was she who had had to yield to my pleas to come ith her from Stillwater and knew how I rebelled against aving her. She may have thought of the chicken as a mforter.

"After all, it's not a big bird."

She immediately made a basket from cloth like the crown a hat with a lid and handle.

"There now, try if he will sit in." The signs by now ere distinctly of a cockerel.

"Yes, he will! He will. I'll tell him to."

I bounded away to tell Aunt Metta that the problem was lved. "Grandma has made a basket for me to carry the icken."

"As if a bird would sit in that!"

153

"He did. We tried!"

"He'll suffocate. Birds smother very easily in warm weather."

It was the hottest time of the year.

"No, he won't! I'll take him out as soon as we are in the train."

"The other passengers may object to being in with a circus troupe," said Aunt Metta in a small but firm voice. "I definitely object."

"Let the child have him," said Grandma. "She won't be a child for long and I may never see her again. If the bird is a trouble you can give it to the guard."

Aunt Metta said no more.

The dreaded day came. I was dressed early and ran away for a last clinging look at what in grander places are known as messuages. It was dire to be torn away in the richest part of the year. The orchards were heavy with ripening fruit. All the old favourites. The fruit of the big apple-tree, the many plums and pears, peaches, mulberries and figs. Grandma's nectarine in her vegetable garden was nearly ready to be rifled, also there was a handsome walnut tree with perfumed foliage, and I would miss the nuts. Grandma's vegetable garden had had to give hospitality to a number of special trees since I had pulled up the seedlings there, and it was now almost an orchard. An annexe had been added for the vegetables. The Hamburg grapes were ripe in purple bunches in the shoulder of the drawingroom fireplace. The sweet-water and white muscatels hung on the dairy veranda at my uncle's. The small Rhine grapes that wreathed a tall plum-tree which I climbed were nearly ready.

Oh, dear, oh, dear! There was not one fruit-tree at Stillwater. Father was labouring like a navvy to make an orchard but the trees would not bear appreciably for three years at least. (This orchard was placed sagely on a slope be safe from flood but the year that it had a nice harvest opening a freak waterspout thunderstorm that raged unmiminished for four hours emptied right on it and washed out a channel that lifted the trees to the fence tops or scattered them for half a mile down on the lower ground.)

I put the chicken in the basket. It fitted him almost as closely as his natal shell. He settled quietly. Well-fed chickens have a habit of pulling up their eyelids like blinds and dozing for extended stretches unless the hen emits a squawk of warning. This one was always contented to be with me, is only means of eating and drinking.

It was a grand far-reaching summer day. As we left, the chicken was a spot of comfort like a dummy nipple to a smaller child. I was so concerned in nursing it that I did not pray wildly to God for something to halt my removal as I had done when four. The incident of the broken doll had relegated prayer to a mere habit.

The chicken was quiescent during the buggy journey. We were to stay at Grandma's cottage in town. Her sister Aunt Mary (owner of the deplorable husband, who had disappeared overseas) lived in some of the rooms. The little town was the coach terminal and a shopping and business centre for the district, like a market town in England. We were to spend two days to pay visits before departing to connect with the branch line which in turn joined the main southern line between Sydney and Melbourne.

Aunt Mary was another beloved of all her nephews and nieces. A year or two later when her sight grew worse and she came to stay with us at Stillwater for months at a stretch, she demonstrated that to love juvenile stories children have to begin young. My junior sisters and brothers hung entranced on the nursery rhymes and stories such as the fate of the three little kittens that lost their mittens. I was so contemptuous and critical of this silly stuff that I was a nuisance. Aunt Mary settled the matter amicably for

155

all by setting me to read to her. I read her several of Dickens's novels without missing a word, wrapped in a possum rug on frosty winter nights flat out on the floor beside Aunt's bed with a candle beside me for light. Neither of us ever tired, so Mother had to intervene to save me. I also read Aunt *Lalla Rookh* and was such a child that I could not be made to waste that *h* and pronounced it "Rookhah" with Aunt's approval. Mother, overhearing, protested,

"I wish you'd correct her pronunciation. She can't be allowed to perpetuate mistakes like that."

"This is a special case between her and me. It will be all right eventually. We understand each other."

It was all right eventually. It was a bond between Aunt and me and has left a pleasant memory.

On the earlier occasion, as I was leaving paradise, she had welcomed the chicken and loosed him with her own fowls. They were amiable. At night I set him near me on newspapers. His disability created interest. All visitors were taken to gaze on him and shown the basket Grandma had made.

"Poor little thing! It's lucky he found such a clever little foster mother."

Aunt Metta alone remained unimpressed. Aunt Mary guarded him while we made calls.

Passengers were hermetically sealed in their carriage between stations, so when coach time drew near Aunt Mary gave me a little bag of food and a bottle of water for the bird. I went for it. He was lying dead on the pathway in the baking sun. A few scout ants had just found him.

It was one of those calamities which in childhood cannot possibly happen, but do. The photographic element in my brain registered details that I did not collate till long afterwards. Aunt Mary was sympathetic. She said her fowls must have attacked him, that fowls were cruel to strangers

r weaker birds. But there was no sign of a struggle, no
loodied head, no ruffled feathers. The chicken lay as
uietly as if asleep just as he had done the day I injured
im, but this time the soft vulnerable form would never
ove again. He had lately been watered: it could not be
nstroke, there was ample shade at hand. Why had the
ther fowls accepted his presence equably during the previ-
us forty-eight hours, to despatch him only when depart-
re was imminent?

The fact of the impossible had to be accepted. I have no
collection of having cried or said anything. It must have
en a shattering blow to one who has never taken lightly
e loss of any friend whether person, animal, bird or tree.
unt Metta could imperceptibly divert any child from fear
naughtiness and probably turned my attention to the
urney.

I always loved the coach with its five and sometimes six
rses. There was the pride of a new dress without a
nafore and a pile of portmanteaux, bandboxes and small
rcels, and the first occasion from which I can recall the
ory of gloves, except riding gauntlets. They are a device
which I am still firmly addicted both for appearance
d cleanliness. The gloves were of thick silk. The day was
t, so were my hands, and the dire struggle to get each
ger completely into its stall was defeated. I was starting
a splendid journey with my adored young aunt. We had
enty of attention, "Such a bright little girl. Like a little
own-up woman." I would be flattered because I was
ith one of the Misses L., famous for their beauty, virtue
d refinement.

The climax of the coach journey was to rumble across a
ng bridge over the Murrumbidgee, the wonder of its age.
hen there was first one train, then another. Trains were
ll of glory and wonder. To sit in a moving house and
ze at trees and hills, to see men on horses like beetles on

far dusty tracks, or ploughing fire-breaks around haystacks, or in a maze of dust with a flock of sheep, was satisfying adventure, and still retains its power to enthrall me.

I don't recall a thought of the chicken, though the gloves with the limp finger ends are vivid in my mind's eye, but its form returned years and years afterwards lying as quietly as if drugged rather than plugged to death. Why after nearly thirty years should it have arisen to haunt? Did Aunt Metta procure some opiate from the chemist to settle the problem of the bird with the broken bill mercifully once for all? This did not occur to me as a possibility till it was too late to ask her to solve the mystery. It remains a puzzle.

In the immediate activity the death of the chicken had no time to coagulate as a tragedy. It was erased by a sense of vaster bereavement in the exile from Eden. I was leaving the place where I had been a child in exceptional circumstances. There I had never suffered discomfort, ill-health, deprivation. There I had known no sordidness, sorrow, humiliation or discontent. Memory refuses to yield even one unmentionable incident or unwholesome secret thought or any despairs, disappointments and anguishes commonly attributed to childhood in similar recollections.

I was going to a life changed in situation and routine, a life more restricted in territory, finances and social association. I had there to encounter and make a place among many new people and children of my own age with whom I had no common inner life. For this rude change I was as lacking in protective worldliness as a bird reared in a boudoir might have been when released to normal living. For one thing I had no knowledge of evil either as sin or vice, nor any understanding that ill-will and unfriendliness could exist.

I was leaving Uncle Hil and my young uncles and aunts and Grandma. I was exchanging their protective aura for

al trials, disappointments and deprivations, and inner grop-
gs and turbulence and furious and agonized beatings of
ings of a bird not knowing where to fly.

Goodbye, young thing, perhaps as much a mirage as a
ality. Go back into the box of imagination and memory
here you belong with those rare people who have retired
that baffling country—the past, lost for ever except in
ese frail inconsequential stories.

Farewell happy childhood!

Appendix—People and places in this book

CHAPTER 1
Father—John Maurice Franklin, born at Yass, N.S.W., 1847.
Mother—Miles Franklin's mother was registered at her birth Margaret Susannah Helena Lampe but on her marriage an death certificates was recorded as Susannah Margaret Eleano She was born at Wambrook station, near Cooma, 1850.
Bobilla—Brindabella station, at the western edge of the presen Capital Territory.

CHAPTER 2
Cousin Joe—Joseph Vallance. His property was named Bramina.

CHAPTER 3
Mother's grandmother—Mrs Wm Bridle (née Martha Miles), bor Prospect, 1807.
Grandmother—Mrs Oltmann Lampe (née Sarah Bridle).

CHAPTER 4
Uncle Hil—William Hilder, m. Agnes Franklin.
Aunt Ignez—Agnes Franklin.
Grandpa—Joseph Franklin of Oakvale, near Yass.

CHAPTER 5
Father's eldest brother—George Franklin.
Ajinby—Talbingo station, at Talbingo.
Mrs H.—Mrs Dan Herlihy.
My second uncle—William Augustus Lampe.
My father's second brother—Thomas Frankiin.

CHAPTER 6
Her [Mrs J. M. Franklin's] father—Oltmann Lampe.
My eldest uncle—John Theodore Lampe.

My youngest uncle—Henry Frederick Lampe.

The surviving dearly loved uncle—William Augustus Lampe. He died 18th June 1959.

A great-uncle—George Bridle.

CHAPTER 7

Mary—Mary Boyd, from Tumut.

Aunt A.—Mrs Thomas Franklin (née Annie McKinnon).

A mountain peak—"Aunt Ignez" is Aunt Agnes (see Chap. 4) and the peak, originally named Mt Agnes, is on the maps now as Mt Aggie.

CHAPTER 8

Gool Gool—Tumut.

Mrs M'G.—Mrs McGregor. She had been a maid at E. K. Crace's station, Gungahleen, Gininderra.

A dashing cousin of Mother's—Edward John Bridle.

CHAPTER 9

Mother's Uncle William; Aunt Lizzie—William Bridle II; his wife, née Elizabeth Margaret Wilkinson.

Aunt Lizzie's two little grand-daughters—Ethel Ruby Bridle and Jessie Emma Bridle, daughters of W. H. Bridle.

A grown-up cousin of Mother's—Lavinia Vernon, daughter of Frederick Vernon and Martha Bridle.

CHAPTER 10

My baby sister—Una Vernon Franklin.

CHAPTER 12

Maurice—John Maurice Franklin, the father of the author.

CHAPTER 14

Polly Wilson—she was a family friend from Adelong.

CHAPTER 16

Grandma's youngest sister—Emma Bridle, m. Frederick Kinred.

CHAPTER 18

Aunt and Uncle—Thomas and Annie Franklin (see notes to Chap. 5, Chap. 7, above).

My eldest girl cousin—Annie May Franklin.

My beautiful little sister—Linda Lampe Franklin.

Our cousins—Annie May, Thomas Ernest, Joseph Michael Edward and George Donald Maurice Franklin.

Cousin A.—Annie May Franklin (Mrs H. E. Bridle).

Don—George Donald Maurice Franklin.

CHAPTER 19
The maid—Mary Boyd.
Our new home—Stillwater, at Thornford, near Goulburn.

CHAPTER 20
My eldest uncle—John Theodore Lampe, m. his cousin Margaret
    Elizabeth Bridle; lived at Woodlands, Talbingo.
The aunt next to him—Mary Martha Bertha Lampe, m. her cousin
    John Wilkinson.

CHAPTER 21
Grandpapa— Oltmann Lampe.
A beautiful aunt of twenty-two years—Emma Elizabeth Lampe,
    born 28th October 1852, died December 1874.
Great grandpapa—Wm Bridle.
The great-aunt who married him late in life—Mary Bridle, m.
    James Gabriel Neal.

CHAPTER 22
My eldest adored maternal uncle—John Theodore Lampe.
Aunt Alice—Alice Helena Lampe.

CHAPTER 23
My favourite brother—Mervyn Gladstone Franklin.
My youngest uncle—Henry Frederick Lampe.

CHAPTER 24
Aunt M.—Sarah Metta Lampe.
Aunt A.—Alice Helena Lampe.

CHAPTER 26
The new grandson—Kenneth Wilkinson.
A grand-daughter of three—Ruby Florence Lampe (Mrs Brydon).
The delightful E.—Ethel Ruby Bridle, daughter of W. H. Bridle.
L.—Lily Martha Kinred, daughter of Fred Kinred and Emma Bridle.

162